Strategic Delegation in Firms
and in the Trade Union

Contributions to Economics

http://www.springer.de/cgi-bin/search_book.pl?series=1262

Guido S. Merzoni

Strategic Delegation in Firms and in the Trade Union

With 3 Figures
and 4 Tables

Physica-Verlag

A Springer-Verlag Company

Series Editors
Werner A. Müller
Martina Bihn

Author

Guido S. Merzoni
Associate Professor of Economics
Facoltà di Scienze Politiche and DISEIS
Università Cattolica del Sacro Cuore
Largo Gemelli, 1
20123 Milano
Italy
merzoni@mi.unicatt.it

ISSN 1431-1933
ISBN 3-7908-1432-6 Physica-Verlag Heidelberg New York

Cataloging-in-Publication Data applied for
A catalog record for this book is available from the Library of Congress.
Bibliographic information published by Die Deutsche Bibliothek
Die Deutsche Bibliothek lists this publication in the Deutsche Nationalbibliografie; detailed bibliographic
data is available in the Internet at <http://dnb.ddb.de>.

Physica-Verlag Heidelberg New York
a member of BertelsmannSpringer Science+Business Media GmbH

© Physica-Verlag Heidelberg 2003
Printed in Germany

Softcover Design: Erich Kirchner, Heidelberg

SPIN 10848866   88/3130/DK-5 4 3 2 1 0 – Printed on acid-free and non-aging paper

To Betty, Giacomo, Alice, Carmela, Sergio and Daniela

Acknowledgements

Most of this book comes from my Ph.D. Thesis at the Department of Economics, University of Warwick. The only exception is the material contained in chapter 4, which comes from a parallel research project whose topic I found particularly suitable to complete the analysis proposed here.

A note of acknowledgement must begin with an expression of my debt to Carlo Beretta, who first introduced me to the study of microeconomics and game theory, inspired my interest in the field and has always encouraged my studies and research.

I would particularly like to thank Norman Ireland and Jonathan Thomas for their precious suggestions and comments while they were supervising my work, as well as Gareth Myles, who did the same at early stages of my thesis.

I have also benefited from comments by my Ph.D. examiners David Ulph and Morten Hviid, Piergiovanna Natale, Flavio Rovida, Gerd Weinrich, five anonymous referees, seminar participants at the 26th Annual Conference of EARIE (Torino, September 1999), the 27th Annual Conference of EARIE (Lausanne, September 2000), the Catholic University of Milan, University of Warwick. My gratitude goes to all of them.

A special thank goes to Michael Luck who helped me with computer simulations.

I would also like to thank Alberto Quadrio Curzio and my colleagues at the Catholic University for having made my journeys to Warwick possible; Luigi Filippini for his encouragement.

Financial support of Fondazione Luigi Einaudi di Torino, IDSE-CNR, ISEIS-Università Cattolica, Consiglio Nazionale delle Ricerche, the European Union under the "Human Capital and Mobility Programme", MURST ex-40% research programme on "Cambiamento strutturale, cambiamento istituzionale e dinamica economica" (chapter 4), MURST ex-40% research programme on "Infrastrutture, competitività, livelli di governo: dall'economia italiana all'economia europea" (chapter 3) is gratefully acknowledged. Finally, MURST research programme "Infrastrutture, competitività, livelli di governo: dall'economia italiana all'economia europea" (1998 - prot.9813030947_002, Catholic University Research Unit) made possible the completion of my research.

I am thankful to Una-Louise Bell, Gianluca Femminis, Humberto Lopez, Michael Luck, Piergiovanna Natale, Flavio Rovida, Oreste Tristani, Guy Vernon for encouraging and helping me in many ways at different stages of the preparation and writing of this work, and to many other friends who have been supporting me even without really being in touch with my research.

I am particularly grateful to Marta, Enrica and Mario Maggioni for their hospitality and friendship, Monica Giulietti and Jeremy Smith for their very patient and friendly personal support and to my wife Betty, my parents, Carmela and Sergio, my sister Daniela, my children Giacomo and Alice for all what they have done and still do for me in so many ways.

October 2002   G. S. Merzoni

Table of contents

Chapter 1 - Introduction

Many economic games are played by delegates, or agents, acting on behalf of their principals, who are the main interested parties.

The relationships between the delegates and their principals, cannot be appropriately discussed within the standard framework of perfectly competitive labour markets, since delegates are supposed to be equipped with decisional and behavioural skills that are not easily transferable to their principals, due to informational asymmetries and lack of observability. Hence, trade in delegates' abilities does not shift the control of resources from the seller to the buyer; rather it consists in a promise to use what remains in control of the seller in the interests of the buyer. As a consequence, hiring an agent implies the delegation to him of a certain degree of discretionary power, so that the relationships between principals and delegates, contrary to what happens in perfectly competitive markets, become personalised: the identity of the person selling the labour service is not irrelevant and the exchange between parties is governed by a set of rules named contract.

Delegation contracts can be explicit or implicit, complete or incomplete. They are explicit when rights and duties of the parties are formally stated, typically in a written document, whereas they are implicit when the relationship is governed by a tacit agreement on what both parties should do. Contracts are complete if they state what both parties should do in each state of nature; they are otherwise incomplete, leaving to the party with the larger bargaining power once the state of nature is revealed, the choice of the terms of exchange in those circumstances.

In this book we concentrate on the analysis of particular principal-delegate relationships, namely those between owners and managers of firms and between members and leaders in unions. However, most of what is said about such relationships is relevant for many other jobs with respect to which buying labour services implies that a certain degree of discretionary power is left to the seller, and where it is not appropriate to treat labour as an homogeneous good. While in economic history there have always been many examples of this kind of relationships, their role has been consistently underplayed in the traditional characterisation of the organisation and social division of labour in industrial societies. The problem has become all the more apparent with the abandonment of Taylorism and standardisation, when this prototype of job implying a delegation of discretionary power has become more and more widespread. Managers and unions leaders are just examples of a much wider phenomenon, in which the relationship between the seller and the buyer of labour services are deeply changed from a non-remote past both outside and within organisations.

The most obvious explanation for the use of delegates is the need of specific competence in playing given games, and so, ultimately, the existence of absolute or comparative advantages, that are exploited to increase the efficiency in the social division of labour.

Another important objective attainable by principals through delegation is the acquisition of a commitment ability, allowing them to render credible strategies that the principal, were she playing, would not be willing to choose. The principal reaches such objective by choosing to be represented by a delegate, whose preferences are different, at the moment when the choice has to be made, from her own: she can either exploit his delegate's personal reputation to be of a certain "type" or shape the delegate's preferences through an explicit, complete and observable incentive contract, or indeed through an incomplete one.

This sort of delegation is known as strategic delegation. The study of its applications to the management of firms and of trade unions is the main purpose of the present book. While in chapters 2 and 3 we study examples of strategic delegation through explicit and complete contracts, in chapter 4 we analyse a case where the strategic effect is obtained through an incomplete contract.

Another issue investigated in this book is the effect on the evolution of market structure of the competition to acquire the best delegates available in the market. The heterogeneity in the distribution of skills makes the market for delegates thin, since, typically, there will not be many delegates with the same skills available at the same time. Hence, it is likely that different principals compete for the same agent. When the activities and interests of principals are interdependent, the contest between them to acquire such a scarce resource has relevant strategic implications on the evolution of their relative market power. In particular, we study whether the dynamic competition between firms to acquire the best managers available in the labour market results in the leading firm increasing its dominance in the product market, or instead allows followers to catch up.

The economic analysis of trade between sellers and buyers of non-standardised labour services has progressed enormously over the last three decades. Most of the papers have concentrated on the provision of incentives through explicit incentive contracts, considering the relationship between a principal and his manager in isolation. However, a vast economic literature has already pointed out that playing through delegates is particularly interesting when the relationship is not considered in isolation and delegation can also be used to gain strategic advantages. Starting from the seminal contribution by Schelling (1960), strategic delegation has been applied to many different economic situations: managerial incentive schemes in oligopolistic market (Vickers, 1985, Fershtman-Judd, 1987, Sklivas, 1987, Macho-Stadler-Verdier, 1991, Basu, 1995), central banks independence (Rogoff, 1985, Persson-Tabellini, 1993, Walsh, 1995), international trade (Gatsios and Karp, 1991), and tax audits (Melumad-Mookherjee, 1989).

The strategic effect of dynamic competition to acquire scarce resources has been studied with reference to patents by Vickers (1986), Delbono (1989), Budd, Harris and Vickers (1993). That literature has shown that the increase in dominance of the leading firm is easier when product markets are more competitive, as for instance in Bertrand oligopolies as opposed to Cournot, and the rise in efficiency due to the acquisition of the new patent is non-drastic. I extend the scope of such analytical setting to consider competition to acquire new managers who become available in the labour market. At difference with such a literature, I also discuss alternative patterns of returns to the amount of the scarce resource available to firms, i.e. managerial skills in my framework.

In this book, it is shown that both in firms and in the Trade Union delegation can, and will, be used by economic agents to gain strategic advantages. When strategic delegation is used by competing firms, a rent-seeking equilibrium might result, in which firms are worse off, but consumers might be advantaged by increased competition. When contracts between principals and agents are observable but renegotiable, they can be used as devices to signal the principals' intention to co-operate. This property of delegation contracts might be used by firms to collude in oligopolistic markets at the consumers' expenses.

Overall, the welfare effects of strategic delegation is uncertain and crucially depends on the features of the model considered. This is true both when delegation is considered in a static framework and when dynamics is introduced.

After the present introductory chapter, in chapter 2 we analyse a model of strategic delegation from owners to managers in a Cournot duopoly where firms compete under incomplete information on the rival marginal costs and the relationships between owners and managers are characterised by moral hazard. It is shown that, despite incomplete information, the owners are able to strategically use the delegation of the output decision by making the managers' explicit and complete incentive contract observable. Strategic delegation enhances the equilibrium level of the managers' effort, decreasing all firms' marginal costs and so increasing expected output. When moral hazard results in under-provision of effort, strategic delegation has a counter-balancing effect on the loss of productivity due to agency costs. In the linear demand case it is also shown that the equilibrium industry output in each state of nature is lower with strategic delegation than otherwise, so that the equilibrium price is distorted toward the monopoly price. Therefore, the expected output increase is all due to the better states of nature becoming more likely. However, at difference from what happens with strategic delegation under complete information in the output setting game, with incomplete information consumers may not benefit from strategic delegation, since consumer's surplus is convex in output.

Chapter 3 begins with the consideration that in the absence of distortions due to agency costs, the strategic use of contracts in delegation games depends on their observability. Observability is usually modelled as a consequence of the principals' ability to fully commit not to renegotiate the contracts they signed. In two slightly different examples of delegation in Cournot duopoly I show that if observability depends on possible renegotiations being observable, the strategic value of contracts is preserved, but the set of equilibria is greatly enlarged. When only one round of perfectly observable renegotiation is allowed, managerial contracts can be used by owners to co-ordinate on any product market equilibrium allowing them to get a level of profit at least as large as the profit obtainable in the strategic delegation equilibrium without renegotiation, which is used as a threat point. When more than one rounds of renegotiations are allowed, renegotiations only become observable to rivals with a short delay and are costly, the equilibrium set includes all the allocations preferred by the owners to Stackelberg leadership. In both examples the equilibrium set includes joint profit maximisation.

In chapter 4 we consider the role of strategic delegation in the relationships between firms and the Trade Union bargaining on workers' wage. We consider in details the organisation of workers interests within unions. The Trade Union is described as an organisation where workers delegate authority, through an incomplete contract, to a leader in order to save on co-ordination costs. These co-ordination costs are due to the difficulties of reaching an agreement among workers and to contracts incompleteness. In particular, we study how different delegation arrangements affect the outcome of wage bargaining. We show that workers may benefit from delegating the authority on wage bargaining to a professional union leader, who does not need to bear directly the costs of industrial actions. Delegation allows the workers to make the threat of using the most effective industrial actions credible, even though those industrial actions are the most costly for the workers themselves. In particular, we consider the choice between going on strike and working to rule. If working to rule is much less effective in damaging the firm and less costly for the workers than going on strike, a union led by a professional will use going on strike as a credible threat. Both the equilibrium wage and the number of employed workers will be higher with the delegation of authority to a professional leader than in the case when workers bargain directly with the firm and the credible threat is working to rule. Our analysis has important implications for the debate on the degree of democracy within the Trade Union. It shows that there is a trade-off between the effectiveness of the union in bargaining and its members' direct participation to the decisional process.

In chapter 5 we study the effect of competition to hire new managers on the evolution of the market structure. Competition for acquiring managers is modelled as a finite sequence of races, where the effect of a new manager on a firm's technology may change with the number of managers previously working for that firm. We prove sufficient conditions for Increasing Dominance, i.e. for the market leader becoming ever more so by attracting all the new available managers, and Catching-Up, i.e. for the follower being able to attract them, and so to gain ground in the product market. Then we study the case of linear Cournot duopoly with differentiated products. It is shown that Increasing Dominance always prevails with both constant and increasing returns to managers, while the outcome of the market evolution with decreasing returns cannot be established in general. However, at difference with what happens in previous models of history dependent races, one can have Catching-Up also in a Cournot duopoly.

Under decreasing returns, the competition for the acquisition of managers increases the likelihood of Catching-Up the lower is the degree of substitutability between the firms' products and the larger is the market size. It causes more frequently Increasing Dominance when the opposite holds. Hence, small and very competitive markets tend to favour the accumulation of human resources in a single, increasingly dominant firm. This equilibrium pattern of evolution certainly hurts consumers, as it is most intuitive, but it is also socially inefficient in many cases.

Chapter 6 summarises the main results.

Chapter 2 - Strategic delegation in firms competing under incomplete information

2.1 Strategic competition and the firm's organisational design

Since the seminal paper by Coase (1937) the firm and the market have been recognised as alternative institutions through which to organise economic activity. However, there is not such a thing as "the firm". Firms are different from each other and their internal organisation should not be taken as an exogenous variable. Furthermore, firms do not exist in isolation; they interact with each other within markets. The structure of the market the firm is operating in influences its internal organisation, and in particular the way in which the incentives for the different parties contributing to the firm activity are designed. This is, of course, especially true when the actions taken by one firm have an influence on the behaviour of its rivals, i.e. in oligopolistic markets, where firms interact strategically. In those circumstances firms can take decisions allowing them to commit to a particular course of action and gain a strategic advantage upon rivals.

Starting with von Stackelberg's (1934), examples of strategic commitment in oligopoly abound in the literature: Spence (1977) and Dixit (1980) on capital investment, Brander & Spencer (1983) on R&D, Schmalensee (1983) on advertising and Fudenberg-Tirole (1983) on learning by doing are just a few, by now almost classic, examples. Fudenberg-Tirole (1984) and Bulow-Geanakoplos-Klemperer (1985) provide a general framework to build a taxonomy of strategic investment. In all these cases the oligopolistic game described is played in two stages. In the second stage each firm makes a choice about either quantity or price. In the first stage at least one of the firms takes an irreversible decision, considering also the effect of that decision on the rivals' behaviour and, as a consequence, on the outcome of the second stage of the game. The irreversibility of the decision taken in the first stage allows the firms to credibly pre-commit to a certain course of action, which will then be taken as given by their rivals. However, all these papers consider "the firm" as the subject taking the strategic decisions and do not account for variety in internal organisation.

Developing on the seminal idea by Schelling (1960), in recent years the so-called "strategic delegation" literature consider the appointment of agents and the provision of incentives for them as pre-commitment devices to be used strategically. A part of this literature focuses on the strategic value of the top managers' incentive schemes in an oligopolistic market (Vickers, 1985, Fershtman-Judd, 1987, Sklivas, 1987, Macho-Stadler-Verdier, 1991, Basu, 1995).[1] These papers provide more examples of strategic commitment in oligopoly, recognising that firms are the result of the interactions of different subjects related to each other through a set of contracts that may be selected strategically. In all these papers in the optimum incentive scheme the remuneration for the manager of an oligopolistic firm competing *à la Cournot* is positively correlated to the firm's total revenues as well as to profits. Through such an incentive scheme, the owner of the firm manipulates the objectives of his manager, committing the firm to an aggressive behaviour in the product market, discouraging rivals and gaining a strategic advantage. This approach emphasises the "external" role of the manager. Managers are described as being representatives appointed just to monitor demand and play the market game. Their objectives can be arbitrarily chosen by the owners. No reference is made to the "internal" role of the manager as the person in charge of the organisation and control of the productive activity. The problem of monitoring their level of effort is not a relevant issue in that framework. The structure of the market does not influence the internal operations and so the efficiency of the firms, but only conditions their selling strategies.

The effect of product market competition on x-inefficiencies caused by asymmetric information in the owner-manager relation has been the main focus of another stream of the literature. These authors investigate the validity of the conventional wisdom view, according to which product

---

[1] Other applications concern the credibility of monetary policy (for example Rogoff (1985) and Lohmann (1992)) or bargaining through agents (Katz (1991)).

market competition disciplines firms, reducing the incidence of agency costs. Hart (1983) shows that the presence of owner-managed firms reduces managerial slack in firms where owners delegate some discretionary power. Scharfstein (1988) points out that Hart's result is sensitive to the assumption he makes of managers' being infinitely risk averse, while different results can be obtained from different assumptions on managerial preferences. Hermalin (1992) shows that the effect of competition on executives' behaviour may be strongly affected by income effects, while the sign of this effect is ambiguous. Martin (1993) gives an example with Cournot competition, which shows that firms efficiency is inversely related to the number of firms in the market. Recently Bertoletti-Poletti (1996) have pointed out that Martin's result is due to a common feature of many of these models, i.e. increasing returns, so that a reduction in the scale of production always reduces the incentives to invest in cost-reducing activities. One of the aims of this chapter is to address the problem of the relations between product market competition and x-inefficiency, and, in particular, to see the effect of strategic delegation on managerial inefficiency.

I present a model of strategic delegation from owners to managers in a Cournot duopoly where firms compete under incomplete information on the rival marginal costs and the relations between owners and managers are characterised by moral hazard. The game has two stages: in the first stage managers' incentive schemes are chosen, while in the second stage the output setting game is played by the managers under incomplete information on the rival's marginal cost. The managers do not only play the output-setting game, but they contribute to the productive activity of the firms through their organisational and monitoring duties, so having a marginal-cost-reducing effect on their firms' activity.

The analysis is meant to verify the validity of the main results of the strategic delegation models, where managers are merely playing the output setting game under perfect information, for this setting where managers, who also contribute to production, select output under incomplete information. With complete information strategic contracting would achieve its commitment effect through a reduction in costs observable to rival firms; with incomplete information this cannot be the case. However, we show that the observability of contracts is enough to accomplish the aim of strategic commitment.

We move, then, to the issues of the effects of strategic contracting and of changes in the degree of product market competition on x-inefficiency.

The basic model with moral hazard and strategic delegation is also compared with alternative settings where the distribution of information and decisional power between owners and managers are different or it is not possible to use incentive contracts as a commitment device. Finally, the effect on consumers' welfare of strategic delegation under incomplete information is evaluated for the linear demand case and compared to what happens in this respect under complete information.

In section 2 the basic structure of the model is presented; in section 3 the equilibrium choices of managers' effort and output are described; in section 4 the equilibrium of the game with strategic delegation is compared with a few alternative settings; section 5 contains the analysis of the linear demand case. Section 6 concludes.

2.2   A model of strategic delegation in duopoly with incomplete information

We consider a duopolistic market with identical firms producing homogeneous goods. Separation between ownership and control prevails. Each firm is owned by a representative individual, the owner, who wants to maximise profits. He delegates to another individual, the manager, the task of running the firm. The activity of the manager usually has an impact on the productivity of the firm. This is taken account of in our model where the manager provides a level of effort which decreases the marginal cost in a way to be made more precise below. The manager exercises his influence in many ways: by monitoring the productive activity, by improving the organisational structure of the firm, by keeping up to date the technology used.

The owner does not observe the manager's level of effort, so that the manager's compensation cannot be made contingent on that. Before the contract is signed, neither player observes the actual level of the marginal cost since some productivity parameter (state of the world) is unknown at this stage (e.g. the quality of inputs, the conditions of the machinery). The manager observes the level of the marginal cost before the output decision is taken. For that reason, each owner delegates the output decision to his manager.

After the decision about output has been made, the owner, as well as any third party, does observe the level of the marginal cost, which provides a signal of the manager's effort. However, the owner never becomes aware of the uncertain productivity parameter, so that the observation of the marginal cost does not reveal to him the level of effort provided by the manager. Nevertheless, a contract in which the manager's compensation is made contingent on the firm's marginal cost is legally enforceable and commits the manager and the owner to its fulfilment, unless they mutually agree otherwise.

Furthermore we assume that the contract is observable. We say that a contract is observable when its contents are known to any third party, who can be sure that it will not be (even secretly) re-negotiated.[2] Observability changes the structure of the game being played, by allowing the player to use the contract for credibly pre-committing to a particular course of action. The assumption of contract observability, while not being by any means innocuous, is widely used in the literature on strategic delegation. For the present case a possible rationale for using it comes from the small number of parties involved in the game.[3] The described situation can be analysed through a multi-stage game, which results from combining a moral hazard principal-agent game with hidden action[4] and a Cournot duopoly game. The timing of the game is the following.

Game 2.1 - Strategic delegation

Stage 1. The owner of each firm offers to his manager a contract, observable to their rivals, which establishes a set of levels of remuneration contingent on the marginal cost that will be observed later: $\left\{\left(w_b, c_b\right),\left(w_g, c_g\right)\right\}$, where the subscript b denotes a bad state of the world (low productivity parameter) and g denotes a good state of the world (high productivity parameter).

Stage 2. Each manager decides whether to accept the offer and, if he does accept, selects his level of effort.

---

[2] For a discussion of the role of observability, see the nexy chapter of this book and Dewatripont (1988).

[3] The fewer are the players, the more they become "visible" to each others, i.e. the easier it becomes to control what is going on in the rival firms.

[4] The classical references for the principal-agent literature are Mirrlees (1975), Holmstrom (1979), Grossman-hart (1983) and Hart-Holmstrom (1987).

Stage 3. Each manager observes his own firm's marginal cost and, having formed his expectations about the rival firm's marginal cost on the basis of the observed contract, chooses the level of output.

Stage 4. Each owner *observes* his own firm's marginal cost and pays the remuneration to his manager.

At both stage 1 and stage 3, the decision-makers have Cournot-Nash conjectures about the rival firm's behaviour.

It may be useful to stress, that the effort level, despite being chosen by the managers, are actually decided by the owners through the choice of the incentive scheme. By representing the principal-agent game as a mere choice of the manager's effort made by the owner, the model may be treated, for simplicity, as a two-stage game with effort determination in the first stage and choice of output in the second. That is what we are going to do in the following sections, after solving for the incentive scheme which implements any given effort level at minimum cost in the present section.

We first consider the principal-agent game.

We assume that the cost structure is stochastic. For simplicity, the marginal cost is either low, at level c_g, with probability $Prob(g)$ or high, c_b, with probability $[1 - Prob(g)]$.[5] The probability distribution of the marginal cost depends on the managers' effort levels e_i and on his ability, described by the parameter α :[6]

$$Prob(g) = \alpha p(e_i) \qquad i=1,2 \tag{2.1}$$

where i stands for the ith firm and $p(e_i)$ is a twice differentiable and strictly concave function. For the problem to make sense $\alpha p(e_i)$ must satisfy the following condition:

$$0 < \alpha p(e_i) < 1 \qquad \forall e_i \tag{2.1a}$$

We assume that, within the range of interest for our problem, the probability of having low costs is non-decreasing in the manager's effort.

---

[5] This formulation with only two possible levels of the outcome of the game follows Grossman and Hart (1983) and Kreps (1990).

[6] Alternatively, α can be interpreted as an industrial sector parameter, which is larger the more intensive is the production technology in manager's effort.

Both the owner and the manager observe this probability distribution over the marginal costs.

The manager's utility function is

$$U = f(w) - xe \tag{2.2}$$

where f is a strictly increasing and twice continuously differentiable function, w is the manager's remuneration and x is a coefficient representing a measure of his "laziness" or disutility of effort, which we will take to be positive. As it is immediately clear by looking at (2.2), the utility function is assumed to be separable in its two arguments. Its first derivatives are

$$\frac{\partial U}{\partial w} > 0$$

$$\frac{\partial U}{\partial e} < 0 .^{7}$$

In our analysis we will consider both risk neutral and risk averse managers.[8]

As mentioned above, the objective of the owner is to maximise profits. He is assumed to be risk neutral.

The owner also knows the manager's utility function and his reservation utility u°.

In order to solve the principal-agent game we split the principal's problem in two parts as suggested by Grossman-Hart (1983). First we find the "best", i.e. the least costly, way to induce the manager to choose a certain level of effort to be determined later; then we calculate the level of the manager's effort preferred by the owner.

The solution of the first part of the owner's problem is the solution of the following constrained cost minimisation problem. For a given e_i

---

[7] The separability assumption implies that the manager's preferences over income are independent of his effort.

[8] Risk averse with respect to the w component.

$$\underset{w_g, w_b}{Min} \quad \alpha p\left(e_i\right)w_g + \left[1 - \alpha p\left(e_i\right)\right]w_b \tag{2.3}$$

s.t.

$$\alpha p\left(e_i\right)f\left(w_g\right) + \left[1 - \alpha p\left(e_i\right)\right]f\left(w_b\right) - xe_i \geq u^\circ \tag{2.4}$$

$$\alpha p'\left(e_i\right)\left[f\left(w_g\right) - f\left(w_b\right)\right] = x \quad ^9 \tag{2.5}$$

As shown by Grossman-Hart (1983), for the preference ordering assumed here, at the optimum both constraints bind. The following conditions for a minimum are found:

$$f\left(w_g\right) - u^\circ - xe_i - \frac{\left[1 - \alpha p\left(e_i\right)\right]x}{\alpha p'\left(e_i\right)} = 0 \tag{2.6}$$

$$f\left(w_b\right) - u^\circ - xe_i + \frac{p\left(e_i\right)x}{p'\left(e_i\right)} = 0 \tag{2.7}$$

Since $f(w)$ is monotonically increasing in w, it has an inverse function $f^{-1}()$. Therefore the solution of the minimisation problem is the following:

(2.4) and (2.5) are the usual participation and incentive constraints. Writing the incentive constraint as in (2.5), we apply the First Order Approach, which can be used since the function $\alpha p(e_i)$ described above satisfies both the Monotone Likelihood Ratio Condition and the Concavity of the Distribution Function Condition (on this see also Jewitt (1988)). Through the incentive constraint (2.5) the solution of the manager's maximisation problem is incorporated in the owner's minimisation problem, whose solution is then a sub-game perfect equilibrium.

$$w_g^* = f^{-1} \left\{ u^\circ + xe_i + \frac{[1 - \alpha p(e_i)]x}{\alpha p'(e_i)} \right\} \qquad (2.8)$$

$$w_b^* = f^{-1} \left\{ u^\circ + xe_i - \frac{p(e_i)x}{p'(e_i)} \right\}^{10} \qquad (2.9)$$

The expected value of the remuneration is:

$$E\left[w^* \left(e_i, \alpha, x, u^\circ \right) \right] = \alpha p(e_i) f^{-1} \left\{ u^\circ + xe_i + \frac{[1 - \alpha p(e_i)]x}{\alpha p'(e_i)} \right\}$$
$$+ [1 - \alpha p(e_i)] f^{-1} \left\{ u^\circ + xe_i - \frac{p(e_i)x}{p'(e_i)} \right\} \qquad (2.10)$$

The manager will get w_g^* if costs are low and w_b^* if costs are high. The incentive scheme in (2.10), which implements any given effort level at minimum cost, is a function of the manager's ability, α, his disutility of effort, x, and his reservation utility, u°. The structure of the game implies that the manager chooses between a set of lotteries. These lotteries differ between each other just for their probability distributions, determined by the level of effort chosen, and not for the size of the prizes (i.e. the levels of remuneration), because w_g^* and w_b^* have already been fixed by the owner when the manager's choice actually occurs.

---

[10] Note that for given w_b^*, w_g^* equations (2.8) and (2.9) can be solved for α and e_i. They are just a rewriting of the two constraints (2.4) and (2.5), that bind in equilibrium. (2.5) has a unique solution for e_i, whenever the two conditions mentioned in the previous footnote are satisfied and so the first-order approach is valid; given (2.5) the left-hand side of (2.4) is monotonically increasing in α, and so has a unique solution for α. Hence the rival manager is able to ascertain the equilibrium level of effort and the ability of firm i's manager only on the basis of the observation of his contract, x, u°, and the knowledge of function $p(e_i)$.

From (2.10) it is easy to see that $E(w*) > f^{-1}(u° + xe_i)$ if $f(w)$ is strictly concave. Therefore, the cost of effort will be larger with asymmetric information than in the case when the owner observes effort and just provides the manager his reservation utility through a fixed remuneration. $E(w*)$ is monotonically increasing in e_i, since

$$\frac{\partial E(w^*)}{\partial e_i} = \alpha p'(e_i)(w_g^* - w_g^*) +$$

$$+ \alpha p(e_i)[1 - \alpha p(e_i)] \frac{xp''(e_i)}{\alpha[p'(e_i)]^2} \left\{ f^{-1} \cdot \left[u° + xe_i - \frac{p(e_i)x}{p'(e_i)} \right] - f^{-1} \cdot \left[u° + xe_i + \frac{(1 - \alpha p(e_i))x}{\alpha p'(e_i)} \right] \right\}$$

(2.10a)

is positive because $p(e_i)$ is concave and $f^{-1}(\cdot)$ is monotonically increasing. It is also easy to see that in order to increase the effort provided by the manager it is necessary to increase the spread between the payments contingent on the two levels of marginal cost, since

$$\frac{\partial w_g^*}{\partial e_i} = -[1 - \alpha p(e_i)] \frac{xp''(e_i)}{\alpha[p'(e_i)]^2} f^{-1} \cdot \left\{ u° + xe_i + \frac{[1 - \alpha p(e_i)]x}{\alpha p'(e_i)} \right\} > 0$$

(2.10b)

while

$$\frac{\partial w_b^*}{\partial e_i} = \alpha p(e_i) \frac{xp''(e_i)}{\alpha[p'(e_i)]^2} f^{-1} \cdot \left\{ u° + xe_i - \frac{\alpha p(e_i)x}{\alpha p'(e_i)} \right\} < 0$$

(2.10c)

However, we cannot generally establish whether the marginal cost of effort is everywhere larger under asymmetric information, so that in equilibrium we might have either under- or over-provision of effort. Furthermore, we cannot generally say anything about the convexity in e_i of $E\left(w^*\right)$; in the analysis that follows for simplicity we assume that $E\left(w^*\right)$ is well-behaved.

2.3   Equilibrium output and effort provision with strategic delegation

So far, only the shape of the incentive scheme which implements any given effort level at minimum cost has been calculated. However, in order to determine the actual value for w_g^* and w_b^*, the owners have to choose the level of the manager's effort they want to implement. This choice completes the effort stage of the game.

We have assumed that each manager's preferences and remuneration scheme are observable. Each manager forms his expectations about the rival's marginal cost on the basis of that observation.[11] Since the managers' effort decreases the probability of their respective firms having a high marginal cost, the choice of the effort level has a strategic value, influencing the outcome of the output-setting game. The owner takes into account that strategic effect of his decision about his manager's effort. The game is solved starting from the output stage and moving backwards. The appropriate solution concept to be used is sub-game perfect equilibrium.

The decision maker in the second stage is the manager of the firm. He is indifferent between the levels of output: hence we assume, as it is often done in the literature, that he will choose in accordance with the owner's will and maximise profits. When he chooses the level of output, the manager observes his own firm's marginal cost and thereby knows what his remuneration is going to be. In his choice, uncertainty enters only with

---

[11] When the managers' contracts are not observable, the analysis proceeds as if the choices concerning the incentive scheme and the level of output were taken simultaneously and no strategic consideration applies. I have analysed the case of unobservable agency contracts with symmetric information about costs in Merzoni (1991). The equilibrium level of effort in that case is the value which minimises total costs.

respect to the rival firm's costs structure. Each manager does not know whether he is playing a high or a low costs firm, i.e. he does not know his opponent's type.

Hence, in this stage we have a game of incomplete information, in which the beliefs depends on the decisions about effort taken in the previous stage. The game is solved as if there were four players, one for each type. The appropriate equilibrium concept to apply is the Bayesian equilibrium. Each manager faces either of two different objective functions according to the level of his firm's marginal cost. Both are weighted sum of the objective functions he would face if he knew the actual value of the rival's marginal cost. The maximisation problem for manager i is:

$$\underset{q_i}{Max} \ \pi_{ig} = \alpha_j \, p\!\left(e_j \right) \left[Y\!\left(q_i, q_{jg} \right) q_i \right] + \left[1 - \alpha_j \, p\!\left(e_j \right) \right] \left[Y\!\left(q_i, q_{jb} \right) q_i \right]$$

$$- w^*_{ig} - c_{ig} q_i$$

$$i, j = 1, 2 \ \ i \neq j \tag{2.11}$$

if the marginal cost is c_{ig} and

$$\underset{q_i}{Max} \ \pi_{ib} = \alpha_j \, p\!\left(e_j \right) \left[Y\!\left(q_i, q_{jg} \right) q_i \right] + \left[1 - \alpha_j \, p\!\left(e_j \right) \right] \left[Y\!\left(q_i, q_{jb} \right) q_i \right]$$

$$- w^*_{ib} - c_{ib} q_i$$

$$i, j = 1, 2 \ \ i \neq j \tag{2.11a}$$

if the marginal cost is c_{ib}.

Here π is the expected profit and $Y\!\left(q_i, q_j \right)$ is the inverse demand function, $\dfrac{\partial Y}{\partial q_i} = \dfrac{\partial Y}{\partial q_j} < 0$.

The simultaneous solutions of the four maximisation problems, two for each player, gives us the Bayesian equilibrium of this stage game. Four first-order conditions like the following are obtained:

$$\frac{\partial \pi_{ig}}{\partial q_i} = \alpha_j p\left(e_j\right)\left[Y'_{q_i}\left(q_i, q_{jg}\right)q_i + Y_{q_i}\left(q_i, q_{jg}\right) - c_{ig}\right]$$

$$+ \left[1 - \alpha_j p\left(e_j\right)\right]\left[Y'_{q_i}\left(q_i, q_{jb}\right)q_i + Y_{q_i}\left(q_i, q_{jb}\right) - c_{ib}\right] = 0$$

(2.12)

The reaction functions for the choice of output made by the four types of firms will be:

$$q_{ig} = \hat{q}_{ig}\left(q_{jg}, q_{jb}, \alpha_j, e_j\right) \qquad i,j = 1,2 \ i \neq j$$

(2.13)

$$q_{ib} = \hat{q}_{ib}\left(q_{jg}, q_{jb}, \alpha_j, e_j\right) \qquad i,j = 1,2 \ i \neq j$$

All the equilibrium values are functions of $\alpha_i, e_i, \alpha_j, e_j$:

$$q_{ig}^* = \hat{\hat{q}}_{ig}\left(\alpha_i, e_i, \alpha_j, e_j\right) \qquad i,j = 1,2 \ i \neq j$$

(2.14)

$$q_{ib}^* = \hat{\hat{q}}_{ib}\left(\alpha_i, e_i, \alpha_j, e_j\right)^{12} \qquad i,j = 1,2 \ i \neq j$$

Therefore the output level of a firm will depend on the effort levels and the ability of its own and the other firm's managers.

Now we move back to the first stage of the game in order to analyse how the managers' effort levels are chosen. When they choose the incentive schemes, the owners do not know their own firms' marginal cost and, as a consequence, which game their managers are playing in the second stage. Therefore, they maximise the following expected profit function,

---

[12] Given the linearity in q of the variable cost function, a sufficient condition for the existence of the equilibrium is that the demand function be weakly concave.

including the two alternative continuations weighted by the objective
probability distribution on them:

$$
\underset{e_i}{Max}\, \pi_i = \alpha_i p(e_i) \left\{ \alpha_j p(e_j) \left[Y\left(q_{ig_i}^*, q_{jg}^* \right) q_{ig}^* \right] + \left[1 - \alpha_j p(e_j) \right] \left[Y\left(q_{ig_i}^*, q_{jb}^* \right) q_{ig}^* \right] \right.
$$

$$
\left. - w_{ig}^* - c_{ig} q_{ig}^* \right\} + \left[1 - \alpha_i p(e_i) \right] \left\{ \alpha_j p(e_j) \left[Y\left(q_{ib_i}^*, q_{jg}^* \right) q_{ib}^* \right] \right.
$$

$$
\left. + \left[1 - \alpha_j p(e_j) \right] \left[Y\left(q_{ib_i}^*, q_{jb}^* \right) q_{ib}^* \right] - w_{ib}^* - c_{ib} q_{ib}^* \right\}
$$

$$
i, j = 1, 2 \;\; i \neq j \tag{2.15}
$$

The simultaneous solution of two maximisation problems like this (one for
each firm) gives us the equilibrium of the effort-setting game. The reaction
functions for the choice of the manager's effort are:

$$
e_i = \hat{e_i}\left(e_j, \alpha_i, \alpha_j \right) \qquad i, j = 1, 2 \;\; i \neq j \tag{2.16}
$$

The equilibrium value for the effort level will be a function of both
managers' ability:

$$
e_i^* = \hat{\hat{e_i}}\left(\alpha_i, \alpha_j \right) \qquad i, j = 1, 2 \;\; i \neq j \tag{2.17}
$$

Through a simple inspection, we note that equation *(2.15)* is just the sum
of the maximum value functions corresponding to the output-setting game
in equations *(2.11)* and *(2.11a)*, weighted by the probability distribution
over the two states of the world. Hence, we can write *(2.15)* as follows:

$$
\underset{e_i}{Max}\;\; \pi_i = \alpha_i p(e_i) \pi_{ig}^* + \left[1 - \alpha_i p(e_i) \right] \pi_{ib}^* \qquad i, j = 1, 2 \;\; i \neq j
$$

$$
\tag{2.18}
$$

Differentiating with respect to e_i we get:

$$\frac{\partial \pi_i}{\partial e_i} = \alpha_i p'(e_i)\left(\pi_{ig}^* - \pi_{ib}^*\right) + \alpha_i p(e_i)\left(\frac{\partial \pi_{ig}^*}{\partial e_i} - \frac{\partial \pi_{ib}^*}{\partial e_i}\right) + \frac{\partial \pi_{ib}^*}{\partial e_i} = 0$$

$$(2.19)$$

where

$$\frac{\partial \pi_{ig}^*}{\partial e_i} = \frac{\partial \pi_{ig}^*}{\partial q_{ig}^*}\frac{\partial q_{ig}^*}{\partial e_i} + \frac{\partial \pi_{ig}^*}{\partial q_{jg}^*}\frac{\partial q_{jg}^*}{\partial e_i} + \frac{\partial \pi_{ig}^*}{\partial q_{jb}^*}\frac{\partial q_{jb}^*}{\partial e_i} - \frac{\partial w_{ig}^*}{\partial e_i} \qquad (2.20a)$$

and

$$\frac{\partial \pi_{ib}^*}{\partial e_i} = \frac{\partial \pi_{ib}^*}{\partial q_{ib}^*}\frac{\partial q_{ib}^*}{\partial e_i} + \frac{\partial \pi_{ib}^*}{\partial q_{jg}^*}\frac{\partial q_{jg}^*}{\partial e_i} + \frac{\partial \pi_{ib}^*}{\partial q_{jb}^*}\frac{\partial q_{jb}^*}{\partial e_i} - \frac{\partial w_{ib}^*}{\partial e_i} \qquad (2.20b)$$

Taking into account that both $\dfrac{\partial \pi_{ig}^*}{\partial q_{ig}^*}$ and $\dfrac{\partial \pi_{ib}^*}{\partial q_{ib}^*}$ are equal to zero for the envelope theorem and substituting *(2.20a)* and *(2.20b)* into *(2.19)* we get:

$$\frac{\partial \pi_i}{\partial e_i} = \alpha_i p'(e_i)\left(\pi_{ig}^* - \pi_{ib}^*\right) + \alpha_i p(e_i)\left(\frac{\partial w_{ib}^*}{\partial e_i} - \frac{\partial w_{ig}^*}{\partial e_i}\right) - \frac{\partial w_{ib}^*}{\partial e_i}$$

$$+ \alpha_i p(e_i)\left(\frac{\partial \pi_{ig}^*}{\partial q_{jg}^*}\frac{\partial q_{jg}^*}{\partial e_i} + \frac{\partial \pi_{ig}^*}{\partial q_{jb}^*}\frac{\partial q_{jb}^*}{\partial e_i}\right) \qquad (2.21)$$

$$+ \left[1 - \alpha_i p(e_i)\right]\left(\frac{\partial \pi_{ib}^*}{\partial q_{jg}^*}\frac{\partial q_{jg}^*}{\partial e_i} + \frac{\partial \pi_{ib}^*}{\partial q_{jb}^*}\frac{\partial q_{jb}^*}{\partial e_i}\right) = 0$$

Equation *(2.21)* characterises the solution of the effort-setting game when the incentive scheme and, as a consequence, the level of effort can be chosen strategically.

2.4   The effort provision under alternative settings

In this section we compare the equilibrium of Game 2.1, with a few alternative settings, where the original model is slightly modified. This allows us to consider the effect on the equilibrium of some of the main features of the model, like the presence of moral hazard, the possibility of delegation and of a strategic use of it, the disciplinary role of product market competition.

2.4.1   No moral hazard

First, we compare the equilibrium of the previous section with the first best with strategic delegation, i.e. with the case when observable managerial contracts can be made contingent on e, since managerial effort is verifiable and so there is no moral hazard. The optimal contract contingent on e provides the manager with just his reservation utility, so that $w_i^* = u^\circ + xe_i$ and the first order condition for the effort setting game is

$$\frac{\partial \pi_i}{\partial e_i} = \alpha_i p'(e_i)\left(\pi_{ig}^* - \pi_{ib}^*\right) + \alpha_i p(e_i)\left(\frac{\partial \pi_{ig}^*}{\partial q_{jg}^*}\frac{\partial q_{jg}^*}{\partial e_i} + \frac{\partial \pi_{ig}^*}{\partial q_{jb}^*}\frac{\partial q_{jb}^*}{\partial e_i}\right)$$

$$+ \left[1 - \alpha_i p(e_i)\right]\left(\frac{\partial \pi_{ib}^*}{\partial q_{jg}^*}\frac{\partial q_{jg}^*}{\partial e_i} + \frac{\partial \pi_{ib}^*}{\partial q_{jb}^*}\frac{\partial q_{jb}^*}{\partial e_i}\right) - x = 0$$

$$(2.22)$$

The effort levels that satisfy *(2.21)* and *(2.22)* are generally different, so that the equilibrium effort of Game 2.1 is not first best; however, as noted above, we cannot generally establish whether *(2.21)* implies under- or over-provision of effort.

2.4.2   Unobservable contracts and non-strategic delegation

Then we move to consider a different setting, where strategic delegation is not an available option, because the contract selected in one firm is not observable by the rival.

Game 2.2 - Unobservable contracts and non-strategic delegation

Stage 1. The owner of each firm offers to his *manager* a contract, not observable to their rivals, which establishes a set of levels of remuneration contingent on the marginal cost that will be observed later: $\left\{ \left(w_b, c_b \right), \left(w_g, c_g \right) \right\}$.

Stage 2. Each manager decides whether to accept the offer and, if he does accept, selects his level of effort.

Stage 3. Each manager observes his own firm's marginal cost and chooses the level of output.

Stage 4. Each owner observes his own firm's *marginal* cost and pays the remuneration to his manager.

As a consequence of contracts being unobservable, in the output setting game each manager rationally foresees that the rival's effort will be the equilibrium effort of the principal-agent game played without taking strategic consideration into account,[13] i.e. solving the following equilibrium condition:

$$\frac{\partial \pi_i}{\partial e_i} = \alpha_i p'\left(e_i\right)\left(\pi_{ig}^* - \pi_{ib}^*\right) + \alpha_i p\left(e_i\right)\left(\frac{\partial w_{ib}^*}{\partial e_i} - \frac{\partial w_{ig}^*}{\partial e_i}\right) - \frac{\partial w_{ib}^*}{\partial e_i}$$

$$= \alpha_i p'\left(e_i\right)\left[\left(R_{ig}^* - R_{ib}^*\right) - \left(q_{ig}^* c_{ig} - q_{ib}^* c_{ib}\right) - \left(w_{ig}^* - w_{ib}^*\right)\right] \qquad (2.23)$$

$$- \alpha_i p\left(e_i\right)\left(\frac{\partial w_{ig}^*}{\partial e_i} - \frac{\partial w_{ib}^*}{\partial e_i}\right) - \frac{\partial w_{ib}^*}{\partial e_i} = 0$$

---

[13] On game played through agents with unobservable contracts, see Katz (1991).

where R_{ig}^* and R_{ib}^* are the expected revenues contingent to respectively the good and the bad state of the world.

Now we are ready to prove the following proposition.

Proposition 2.1. If the products of the two firms are strategic substitutes and the equilibrium level of output decreases in the rival manager's effort, strategic delegation implies an equilibrium level of effort larger than in the case of non-strategic delegation.

Proof. By comparing equations *(2.21)* and *(2.23)* we notice that *(2.21)* contains the following extra term:

$$\alpha_i p(e_i)\left(\frac{\partial \pi_{ig}^*}{\partial q_{jg}^*}\frac{\partial q_{jg}^*}{\partial e_i}+\frac{\partial \pi_{ig}^*}{\partial q_{jb}^*}\frac{\partial q_{jb}^*}{\partial e_i}\right)+\left[1-\alpha_i p(e_i)\right]\left(\frac{\partial \pi_{ib}^*}{\partial q_{jg}^*}\frac{\partial q_{jg}^*}{\partial e_i}+\frac{\partial \pi_{ib}^*}{\partial q_{jb}^*}\frac{\partial q_{jb}^*}{\partial e_i}\right).$$

This is positive because the products are strategic substitutes and the levels of output decrease in the rival's effort. Therefore, for concavity of π_i in e_i, e_i^* is greater when delegation is strategic than otherwise. (Q.E.D.)

Therefore, when the owner of one firm is able to use strategically his manager's incentive contract, he will select, caeteris paribus, an equilibrium level of effort higher than otherwise, decreasing the expected level of marginal cost. However, it is important to notice that strategic delegation equilibrium implies a level of the manager's effort that does not minimise total costs, as it would be the case were the owner deciding.

2.4.3   No delegation

By delegating the output decision to his manager, the owner takes advantage of the manager's capability to distinguish between different states of nature in order to increase revenues. When the choice of output cannot be delegated, so that the firm is owner-managed and the agent we have called "manager" so far only acts as a supervisor of production, the game becomes the following.

Game 2.3 - Owner-managed firm (no delegation)

Stage 1. The owner of each firm offers to the supervisor of production a contract, not observable to their rivals, which establishes a set of levels of remuneration contingent on the marginal cost that will be observed later: $\left\{ \left(w_b, c_b \right), \left(w_g, c_g \right) \right\}$.

Stage 2. Each supervisor decides whether to *accept* the offer and, if he does accept, selects his level of effort.

Stage 3. Each owner selects output, before *observing* the realisation of marginal cost.

Stage 4. Each owner observes his own firm's marginal cost and pays the remuneration to his supervisor.

In this case the f.o.c. for the effort-setting game only implies total expected costs minimisation, since the level of effort does not have any effect on the choice of output, apart from that going through the expected value of marginal cost:

$$\frac{\partial \pi_i}{\partial e_i} = -\alpha_i p'\left(e_i\right)\left[\left(w_{ig}^* - w_{ib}^*\right)\right] - \alpha_i p\left(e_i\right)\left(\frac{\partial w_{ig}^*}{\partial e_i} - \frac{\partial w_{ib}^*}{\partial e_i}\right)$$

$$-\frac{\partial w_{ib}^*}{\partial e_i} - \alpha_i p'\left(e_i\right)q_i^*\left(c_{ig} - c_{ib}\right) = 0$$

$$(2.24)$$

As a term of comparison we consider the game with non-strategic delegation and re-write for convenience the f.o.c. for that case:

$$\frac{\partial \pi_i}{\partial e_i} = \alpha_i p'\left(e_i\right)\left[\left(R_{ig}^* - R_{ib}^*\right) - \left(q_{ig}^* c_{ig} - q_{ib}^* c_{ib}\right)\right] - \alpha_i p'\left(e_i\right)\left[\left(w_{ig}^* - w_{ib}^*\right)\right]$$

$$-\alpha_i p\left(e_i\right)\left(\frac{\partial w_{ig}^*}{\partial e_i} - \frac{\partial w_{ib}^*}{\partial e_i}\right) - \frac{\partial w_{ib}^*}{\partial e_i} = 0$$

$$(2.23)$$

Now we are ready to prove the following proposition.

Proposition 2.2. The delegation of the output decision to an informed manager implies a higher equilibrium level of effort than the corresponding case without delegation.

Proof. By comparing equation *(2.23)* and *(2.24)*, we notice that the left hand side of *(2.23)* is larger than the left hand side of *(2.24)*, since the difference in profit gross of the manager's remuneration between the good and the bad state of nature when an informed manager chooses q_i exceed the difference in production costs between the two state when a uninformed owner makes the decision. The result follows from concavity of the expected profit function. (Q.E.D.)

Therefore, the use of delegation enhances the profitability of decreasing the firm's marginal cost. As a consequence the equilibrium level of marginal cost decreases.

The fact that the level of effort of one firm's manager increases when his incentive scheme is used strategically or delegation takes place, does not necessarily mean that the same happens for all firms in the industry, when all the owners behave in the same way. When the levels of effort are strategic substitutes, as we have assumed for Proposition 2.1, the outcome will depend on which between the own and the cross effect prevails. Proposition 2.3, which follows the line of reasoning of the paper by Brander and Spencer (1983) on R&D rivalry, states the conditions for the net effect to be positive.[14]

Proposition 2.3. If the firms are symmetric and the equilibrium in the effort setting game is stable:

- the equilibrium level of effort of each firm's manager in the strategic delegation game is greater than in the non-strategic one;

- the equilibrium level of effort of each firm's manager in the game with delegation is greater than without delegation.

Proof. (see Appendix 2.1).

Therefore strategic and non-strategic delegation decrease the expected level of marginal cost of all the firms in the industry.

---

[14] They consider the duopoly case, but the main result extend to oligopolies with more than two firms.

2.4.4   Product market competition and agency costs

Before closing this section we add a final remark on the relations between product market competition, strategic delegation and agency costs. The literature does not always provide support to the conventional wisdom argument, according to which product markets discipline firms, so reducing agency costs.[15] In our framework the second best equilibrium of the moral hazard game described in section 2 implies a distortion in the level of effort, whose sign cannot be unequivocally established, so that we might have either under- or over-provision of effort. When moral hazard implies under-provision of effort, Proposition 2.3 has an important corollary: strategic delegation tends to counterbalance the x-inefficiency due to agency costs.

Corollary 2.4. In a duopolistic market where the products are strategic substitutes, strategic delegation of the output decision to a manager reduces the under-provision of managerial effort due to moral hazard, if that occurs.

Finally, we investigate how the equilibrium effort is affected by whether or not the firms relax product market competition by colluding to fully extract the potential joint surplus of the market. The f.o.c. for the choice of effort of a colluding firm would be

$$\frac{\partial \pi_i}{\partial e_i} = \alpha_i p'(e_i) \left[\left(\pi_{ig}^c - \pi_{ib}^c \right) \right] - \alpha_i p(e_i) \left(\frac{\partial w_{ig}^*}{\partial e_i} - \frac{\partial w_{ib}^*}{\partial e_i} \right) - \frac{\partial w_{ib}^*}{\partial e_i} = 0$$

$$(2.25)$$

where π_{ig}^c and π_{ib}^c are the profit of collusion when the marginal costs are respectively low and high. If we compare *(2.25)* with the f.o.c. of the game with strategic delegation *(2.21)*, we notice that *(2.21)* contains the same extra-term as for the case of non-strategic delegation. In fact, colluding firms have no incentive to over-invest to discourage rivals.

---

[15] As noticed in the introduction, this problem is discussed in different settings by Hart (1983), Scharfstein (1988), Hermalin (1992), Martin (1993), Bertoletti and Poletti (1996).

Furthermore, in *(2.25)* we have $\alpha_i\, p'(e_i)\left[\left(\pi^c_{ig} - \pi^c_{ib}\right)\right]$ in place of $\alpha_i\, p'(e_i)\left[\left(\pi^*_{ig} - \pi^*_{ib}\right)\right]$ in *(2.21)*. Then, we can establish the following lemma.

Lemma 2.5. The equilibrium level of effort of the managers is lower when firms collude than without collusion if

$$\alpha_i\, p'(e_i)\left[\left(\pi^c_{ig} - \pi^c_{ib}\right)\right] < \alpha_i\, p'(e_i)\left[\left(\pi^*_{ig} - \pi^*_{ib}\right)\right].$$

Proof. If $\alpha_i\, p'(e_i)\left[\left(\pi^c_{ig} - \pi^c_{ib}\right)\right] < \alpha_i\, p'(e_i)\left[\left(\pi^*_{ig} - \pi^*_{ib}\right)\right]$ the left hand side of *(2.25)* is always smaller than the left hand side of *(2.21)*. The result follows from concavity of the profit function. (Q.E.D.)

A simple setting where the condition in Lemma 2.5 is satisfied is the case of linear demand with symmetric costs, as shown in the following section. Lemma 2.5 shows that when agency costs imply under-provision of effort, an increase of competitiveness of the product market, represented by the removal of collusion, disciplines firms and reduces x-inefficiencies.

2.5   The case of linear demand

In order to get some further insights, we consider the simple case of linear demand:

$$Y\left(q_i, q_j\right) = a - q_i - q_j. \tag{2.26}$$

The first order conditions for firm *i* in the two states of nature are

$$\frac{\partial \pi_{ig}}{\partial q_i} = \alpha_j\, p\left(e_j\right)\left(a - 2q_{ig} - q_{jg} - c_{ig}\right)$$

$$+ \left[1 - \alpha_j\, p\left(e_j\right)\right]\left(a - 2q_{ig} - q_{jb} - c_{ig}\right) = 0$$

$$\tag{2.27}$$

$$\frac{\partial \pi_{ib}}{\partial q_i} = \alpha_j p\left(e_j\right)\left(a - 2q_{ib} - q_{jg} - c_{ib}\right)$$

$$+ \left[1 - \alpha_j p\left(e_j\right)\right]\left(a - 2q_{ib} - q_{jb} - c_{ib}\right) = 0$$

Hence, the reaction functions are:

$$q_{ib} = \frac{a - c_{ig} - \alpha_j p\left(e_j\right)q_{jg} + \left[1 - \alpha_j p\left(e_j\right)\right]q_{jb}}{2}$$

$$(2.28)$$

$$q_{ib} = \frac{a - c_{ib} - \alpha_j p\left(e_j\right)q_{jg} + \left[1 - \alpha_j p\left(e_j\right)\right]q_{jb}}{2}$$

which are linear in the expected value of the rival's output.

Figure 2.1 below illustrates the situation facing the manager of firm i's when he plays the output setting game, $c_i = c_{ig}$ and he is uncertain on the actual value of firm j's cost between c_{jg} and c_{jb}.

The equilibrium output of firm i depends on its manager's expectations on the value of q_j and will be in the interval between $\underline{q_{ig}}$ and $\overline{q_{ig}}$.

Straightforward comparative statics on the reaction functions shows that the output of both firms in all states of nature are inversely related to the rival manager's ability and effort.

Figure 2.1: Reaction functions for the output setting game

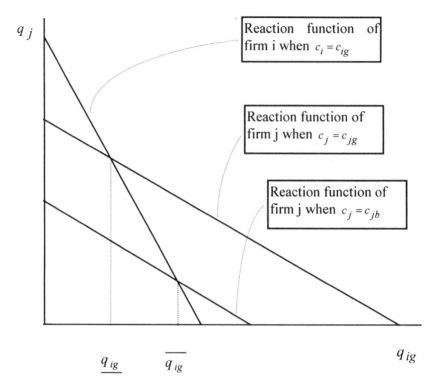

The equilibrium values for the output-setting game are the following:

$$q_{ig}^* = \frac{a + \alpha_i p\left(e_i\right)\left(\dfrac{c_{ib} - c_{ig}}{2}\right) - \dfrac{1}{2}c_{ib} - \dfrac{3}{2}c_{ig} - 2\alpha_j p\left(e_j\right)\left(\dfrac{c_{jb} - c_{jg}}{2}\right) + c_{jb}}{3}$$

(2.29a)

$$q_{ib}^* = \frac{a + \alpha_i \, p\big(e_i\big)\left(\dfrac{c_{ib} - c_{ig}}{2}\right) - 2c_{ib} - 2\alpha_j \, p\big(e_j\big)\left(\dfrac{c_{jb} - c_{jg}}{2}\right) + c_{jb}}{3}$$

(2.29b)

The explicit solution of the output-setting game allows us to prove the three following Lemmas.

Lemma 2.6. If the demand is linear, the managers' effort levels are strategic substitutes.

Proof. (see Appendix 2.1).

Lemma 2.7. If the demand is linear, a rise in the manager's effort increases the equilibrium levels of output of his own firm and decreases the levels of output of the rival.

Proof. Direct from *(2.29a)* and *(2.29b)*.

Lemma 2.7 shows that the linear demand case satisfies the conditions for Proposition 2.1 to hold.

Lemma 2.8. If the demand is linear, a rise in the manager's ability increases the equilibrium levels of output of his own firm and decreases the levels of output of the rival.

Proof. Direct from *(2.29a)* and *(2.29b)*.

Lemma 2.8 shows the consequences of the choice of the manager's ability on his own and the rival firm's behaviour. In particular, given the existence of a negative cross effect, we can see that also the choice of the manager's ability can be used strategically.

Then, we consider the total effect on expected output of the strategic behaviour of both firms. For Proposition 2.3 we know that the equilibrium level of effort of both firms is greater when they behave strategically than otherwise. Hence, in order to evaluate the whole effect of the strategic behaviour on total industry expected output is enough to inspect the effect of a change in just one firm's manager effort level.

Proposition 2.9. If the demand is linear, when all firms choose their manager's effort strategically, the expected total industry output increases.

Proof. From (2.29a) and (2.29b) it is easy to see that

$$\frac{\partial E\left(q_i^*\right)}{\partial e_i} + \frac{\partial E\left(q_j^*\right)}{\partial e_i} = \alpha_i\, p'\!\left(e_i\right)\left[\frac{2\left(c_{ib} - c_{ig}\right)}{3} - \frac{\left(c_{ib} - c_{ig}\right)}{3}\right]$$

$$= \alpha_i\, p'\!\left(e_i\right)\left(\frac{c_{ib} - c_{ig}}{3}\right) > 0 \tag{2.30}$$

The same holds for the change in e_j.

Since the net result of the strategic behaviour of both firms is an increase in both e_i and e_j, the total variation in the industry output will be positive (Q.E.D.).

It is interesting to note that in the symmetric case, when $c_{ig} = c_{jg}$, $c_{ib} = c_{jb}$ and $\alpha_j = \alpha_i$, the expected output increase due to strategic over-investment in effort depends on the good state of nature becoming more likely, while in each state the equilibrium output is lower for both firms. This is implied by the following lemma.

Lemma 2.10. In the symmetric case, if the demand is linear, the equilibrium output in each state of nature is smaller when the managers' effort levels are chosen strategically than otherwise.

Proof. From (2.29a) and (2.29b) we know that

$$\frac{\partial q_{ig}^*}{\partial e_i} + \frac{\partial q_{ig}^*}{\partial e_j} = \frac{\alpha_i\, p'\!\left(e_i\right)\dfrac{\left(c_{ib} - c_{ig}\right)}{2} - 2\alpha_j\, p'\!\left(e_j\right)\left(\dfrac{c_{jb} - c_{jg}}{2}\right)}{3}$$

$$\tag{2.31}$$

In the symmetric case this simplifies to

$$\frac{\partial q^*_{ig}}{\partial e_i} + \frac{\partial q^*_{ig}}{\partial e_j} = -\frac{\alpha p'(e)\left(\dfrac{c_b - c_g}{2}\right)}{3} < 0. \tag{2.32}$$

We have already shown that equilibrium effort levels are larger in the strategic equilibrium than otherwise. Therefore, q^*_{ig} is smaller in the strategic equilibrium than otherwise. The same holds for q^*_{ib}, q^*_{jg} and q^*_{jb}. (Q.E.D.)

In the strategic delegation case the equilibrium output in each state of nature is lowered by the increase in the expectations that the rival is in the good state due to the observation of a contract that implies over-investment in effort. This forces the managers to exercise restraint and reduce the output their firms produce. Given the reduction in output in each state of nature, the increase in the expected level of output in the strategic delegation case entirely depends on the increased probability of being in the good states.

An immediate corollary of Lemma 2.10 is the following.

Corollary 2.11. In a Cournot duopoly with incomplete information the equilibrium price in each state of nature will be higher in the strategic delegation equilibrium than otherwise, i.e. it will be pushed towards monopoly price.

When the realisation of the shocks on costs in the two firms is the same, this directly implies that total revenues gross of managerial compensation are higher in both firms; while the effect on profit is ambiguous.

The effect of strategic delegation on consumer welfare is also ambiguous. We have shown that total industry expected output is higher in the strategic delegation equilibrium than otherwise. However, total output in each state of nature is lower, while with linear demand consumer surplus is convex in output.

The present framework of incomplete information in the output setting game and related results are to be compared with models of strategic delegation under complete information like those in Fershtman-Judd (1987) and Sklivas (1987). In those models strategic delegation with

Cournot competition increases the equilibrium output and so decreases the equilibrium price and consumer surplus. We have seen that under incomplete information the reverse may hold.

Finally, we can easily show that with linear demand the condition in Lemma 2.5 is satisfied in the symmetric case, and so collusion has an effort-reducing effect on managers.

Lemma 2.12. If the demand is linear and costs are symmetric

$$\alpha_i p'(e_i)\left[\left(\pi_{ig}^c - \pi_{ib}^c\right)\right] < \alpha_i p'(e_i)\left[\left(\pi_{ig}^* - \pi_{ib}^*\right)\right].$$

Proof. When marginal costs are symmetric the most obvious division of market shares between colluding firms would allocate half of the production to each. Each firm's profit would be half of the monopoly profit. When demand is like in (2.26), the derivative of firm i's profit with respect to c_i in the symmetric case is:

$$\frac{\partial \pi_i^*}{\partial c_i} = -\frac{4}{9}\left(a - 2c_i + c_j\right) = -\frac{4}{9}\left(a - c\right) \tag{2.33}$$

without collusion and

$$\frac{\partial \pi_i^c}{\partial c_i} = -\frac{1}{4}\left(a - c\right) \tag{2.34}$$

with collusion. Hence the variation in profit due to a shift from a bad to a good state of nature is smaller with collusion than otherwise. (Q.E.D.)

2.6   Conclusions

In this chapter we have shown that despite incomplete information in the product market the owners are able to use strategically the delegation of the output decision to managers by merely making the managers' incentive schemes observable. Strategic delegation enhances the equilibrium level of the managers' effort, decreasing all firms' marginal costs. Equilibrium effort with strategic delegation is above that minimising each firm's total cost, the level which would be selected with no delegation, i.e. were the owner playing the product market game without the manager's intermediation.

Moral hazard is another source of distortion of the equilibrium effort, which can generate under- but also over-provision of effort. When the former is the case, strategic delegation has a counter-balancing effect on the loss of productivity due to agency costs. Also, an increase in the degree of competitiveness of the product market, represented by the elimination of collusion, increases equilibrium effort and then have similar effect on agency distortions.

The analysis of the linear demand case has allowed us to show some interesting features of the strategic delegation equilibrium under incomplete information. The expected value of the equilibrium industry output is higher with strategic delegation than otherwise; however, the equilibrium industry output in each state of nature is lower, so that the equilibrium price is distorted toward the monopoly price. Therefore, the expected output increase is all due to the better states of nature becoming more likely. However, at difference with what happens with strategic delegation under complete information in the output setting game, in this model consumers may not benefit from strategic delegation, since consumer's surplus is convex in output.

Appendix 2.1. Proofs of Proposition 2.3 and of Lemma 2.6

Proof of Proposition 2.3. As in Brander and Spencer (1983), in order to compare strategic and non-strategic equilibria, we apply the mean value theorem. We start writing the following expression, showing the two components of the total variation in $\dfrac{\partial \pi_i}{\partial e_i}$ caused by a shift from the non-strategic to the strategic delegation equilibrium:

$$\Delta \frac{\partial \pi_i}{\partial e_i} = \frac{\partial^2 \pi_i}{\partial e_i^2} \Delta e_i + \frac{\partial^2 \pi_i}{\partial e_i \partial e_j} \Delta e_j \qquad (2.\text{A}1)$$

where Δ indicates any difference between the strategic and the non-strategic equilibrium. The same kind of expression can be written for

$\dfrac{\partial \pi_i}{\partial e_j}$, so that we obtain a two equations system, which is solved for Δe_i

and Δe_j Adding the two expressions obtained we get

$$\Delta e_i + \Delta e_j = \dfrac{\left(\dfrac{\partial^2 \pi_i}{\partial e_i^2} - \dfrac{\partial^2 \pi_i}{\partial e_i \partial e_j}\right) \Delta \dfrac{\partial \pi_j}{\partial e_j} + \left(\dfrac{\partial^2 \pi_j}{\partial e_j^2} - \dfrac{\partial^2 \pi_j}{\partial e_j \partial e_i}\right) \Delta \dfrac{\partial \pi_i}{\partial e_i}}{\dfrac{\partial^2 \pi_i}{\partial e_i^2} \dfrac{\partial^2 \pi_j}{\partial e_j^2} - \dfrac{\partial^2 \pi_i}{\partial e_i \partial e_j} \dfrac{\partial^2 \pi_j}{\partial e_j \partial e_i}}$$

$$(2.A2)$$

The denominator in *(2.A2)* is positive, being the determinant of the Jacobian matrix for the profit maximisations of the two firms. Furthermore, for local stability and symmetry $\dfrac{\partial^2 \pi_i}{\partial e_i^2} < \dfrac{\partial^2 \pi_i}{\partial e_i \partial e_j}$ and

$\dfrac{\partial^2 \pi_j}{\partial e_j^2} < \dfrac{\partial^2 \pi_j}{\partial e_j \partial e_i}$.

$\Delta \dfrac{\partial \pi_i}{\partial e_i}$ and $\Delta \dfrac{\partial \pi_j}{\partial e_j}$ remain to be signed. $\Delta \dfrac{\partial \pi_i}{\partial e_i}$ can be written as the

difference between the value of $\dfrac{\partial \pi_i}{\partial e_i}$ at the strategic $\dfrac{\partial \pi_i}{\partial e_i^s}$ and at the non-

strategic equilibrium $\dfrac{\partial \pi_i}{\partial e_i^n}$:

$$\Delta \dfrac{\partial \pi_i}{\partial e_i} = \dfrac{\partial \pi_i}{\partial e_i^s} - \dfrac{\partial \pi_i}{\partial e_i^n}. \qquad (2.A3)$$

The first term on the right-hand side is zero for profit maximisation, while $\dfrac{\partial \pi_i}{\partial e_i^n}$ is positive, since at e_i^n the strategic distortion is not taken into account in the maximising choice. The same holds for $\Delta \dfrac{\partial \pi_j}{\partial e_j}$. Therefore, (2.A2) is positive. In much the same way (2.A2) is shown to be positive for a change from an equilibrium without delegation to an equilibrium with delegation (Q.E.D.).

Proof of Lemma 2.6. If the managers' effort levels are strategic substitutes, the reaction functions for the effort-setting game must be downward sloping:

$$\frac{\partial e_i}{\partial e_j} = \frac{\dfrac{\partial^2 \pi_i}{\partial e_i \partial e_j}}{\dfrac{\partial^2 \pi_i}{\partial e_i^2}} < 0. \tag{2.A4}$$

We know that $\dfrac{\partial^2 \pi_i}{\partial e_i^2}$ is negative, being a second-order condition for profit maximisation, while $\dfrac{\partial^2 \pi_i}{\partial e_i \partial e_j}$ remains to be signed. In the linear demand case, taking into account that $\dfrac{\partial Y}{\partial q_{jb}} = \dfrac{\partial Y}{\partial q_{jg}} = \dfrac{\partial Y}{\partial q_j}$ and $\dfrac{\partial q_{jb}}{\partial e_i} = \dfrac{\partial q_{jg}}{\partial e_i} = \dfrac{\partial q_j}{\partial e_i}$, $\dfrac{\partial \pi_i}{\partial e_i}$ may be written as follows:

$$\frac{\partial \pi_i}{\partial e_i} = \alpha_i p'(e_i)\left(\pi_{ig}^* - \pi_{ib}^*\right) + \left\{\alpha_i p(e_i)\left(q_{ig}\frac{\partial Y}{\partial q_j}\frac{\partial q_j}{\partial e_i} - q_{ib}\frac{\partial Y}{\partial q_j}\frac{\partial q_j}{\partial e_i} - \frac{\partial w_{ig}^*}{\partial e_i} + \frac{\partial w_{ib}^*}{\partial e_i}\right)\right.$$

$$\left. + q_{ib}\frac{\partial Y}{\partial q_j}\frac{\partial q_j}{\partial e_i} - \frac{\partial w_{ib}^*}{\partial e_i}\right\}$$

$$\tag{2.A5}$$

Therefore,

$$
\frac{\partial^2 \pi_i}{\partial e_i \partial e_j} = \alpha_i p'(e_i) \left(\frac{\partial \overset{*}{\pi}_{ig}}{\partial e_j} - \frac{\partial \overset{*}{\pi}_{ib}}{\partial e_j} \right) + \left\{ \alpha_i p(e_i) \left(\frac{\partial q_{ig}}{\partial e_j} \frac{\partial Y}{\partial q_j} \frac{\partial q_j}{\partial e_i} - \frac{\partial q_{ib}}{\partial e_j} \frac{\partial Y}{\partial q_j} \frac{\partial q_j}{\partial e_i} \right. \right.
$$

$$
\left. \frac{\partial^2 \overset{*}{w}_{ig}}{\partial e_i \partial e_j} + \frac{\partial^2 \overset{*}{w}_{ib}}{\partial e_i \partial e_j} \right) \frac{\partial q_{ib}}{\partial e_j} \frac{\partial Y}{\partial q_j} \frac{\partial q_j}{\partial e_i} - \frac{\partial^2 \overset{*}{w}_{ib}}{\partial e_i \partial e_j} \right\}
$$

(2.A6)

From (2.8) and (2.9) we know that $\dfrac{\partial^2 \overset{*}{w}_{ig}}{\partial e_i \partial e_j} = \dfrac{\partial^2 \overset{*}{w}_{ib}}{\partial e_i \partial e_j} = 0$, while from

(2.29a) and (2.29b) we know that $\dfrac{\partial q_{ig}}{\partial e_j} \dfrac{\partial Y}{\partial q_j} \dfrac{\partial q_j}{\partial e_i} = \dfrac{\partial q_{ib}}{\partial e_j} \dfrac{\partial Y}{\partial q_j} \dfrac{\partial q_j}{\partial e_i} < 0$.

Furthermore, in the linear demand case, given that $\dfrac{\partial q_{jg}}{\partial e_j} = \dfrac{\partial q_{jb}}{\partial e_j}$, the

following hold

$$
\frac{\partial \overset{*}{\pi}_{ig}}{\partial e_j} = \alpha_j p'(e_j) \left\{ \left[Y\left(\overset{*}{q}_{ig}, q_{jg} \right) \overset{*}{q}_{ig} - \overset{*}{w}_{ig} - c_{ig} \overset{*}{q}_{ig} \right] \right.
$$

$$
\left. - \left[Y\left(\overset{*}{q}_{ig}, q_{jb} \right) \overset{*}{q}_{ig} - \overset{*}{w}_{ig} - c_{ig} \overset{*}{q}_{ig} \right] \right\}
$$

(2.A7)

$$
\frac{\partial \overset{*}{\pi}_{ib}}{\partial e_j} = \alpha_j p'(e_j) \left\{ \left[Y\left(\overset{*}{q}_{ib}, q_{jg} \right) \overset{*}{q}_{ib} - \overset{*}{w}_{ib} - c_{ib} \overset{*}{q}_{ib} \right] \right.
$$

$$
\left. - \left[Y\left(\overset{*}{q}_{ib}, q_{jb} \right) \overset{*}{q}_{ib} - \overset{*}{w}_{ib} - c_{ib} \overset{*}{q}_{ib} \right] \right\}
$$

(2.A8)

The difference between $\dfrac{\partial \pi^{*}_{ig}}{\partial e_{j}} - \dfrac{\partial \pi^{*}_{ib}}{\partial e_{j}}$ is negative, since $\dfrac{\partial^{2} \pi_{i}}{\partial q_{i} \partial q_{j}} < 0$

for output being strategic substitutes and then the variation in expected profit of firm i due to a change in q_{i} when firm j is in the bad state of nature is greater than the corresponding change when firm j is in the good state of nature. Therefore, (2.A6) is negative and (2.A4) is negative as well (Q.E.D.).

Chapter 3 - Delegation contracts' observability and collusion

3.1   Introduction[*]

Co-operation is easier to attain, when the players are able to observe each other. Contracts, like other institutions, can be used by economic agents to become more observable, state their intentions and define their role. In this chapter, we analyse the possibility that incentive contracts for delegates could be used by principals to sustain co-operation, studying an application to Cournot oligopoly. It is shown that collusion is a sub-game perfect equilibrium of a Cournot duopoly game between two firms, where, as in the previous chapter, the choice of output is delegated by each owner to a manager, and the managers' incentive schemes are observable and renegotiable.

This result is in contrast with most of the previous literature on Cournot oligopoly with strategic delegation and with the results of the previous chapter, which suggest that the market equilibrium in this kind of framework tends to be very competitive, because the owners use the incentive schemes for discouraging rivals (Vickers, 1985, Fershtman-Judd, 1987, Sklivas, 1987, Basu, 1995).

The main exception to all these is Fershtman-Judd-Kalai (1991).[1] In that paper, collusion is implemented by means of target contracts which force

[*] A previous version of this chapter was presented at the 26th Annual Conference of EARIE in Turin, 4-7 September 1999. This research was partially carried out within the MURST ex-40% project on "Infrastrutture, competitività, livelli di governo: dall'economia italiana all'economia europea".

the managers to choose the collusive level of output and to punish the rival owner if he deviates in setting his manager's contract. So, managerial incentive schemes are almost open commitment to collusion, easy to be detected by any interested third party.[2] Furthermore, target contracts do not seem robust to changes in the model's setting, and particularly to the introduction of uncertainty. Finally, Fershtman, Judd and Kalai assume that owners and managers can fully commit not to renegotiate the contract even if they both could benefit from doing so. This assumption, while being frequently used, seems to be very strong and somehow at odds with what one would expect in real life situation, as it will be argued in section 2.

In this chapter, collusive contracts do not openly target collusion, but give to the managers an incentive to weight costs more than the owners. Renegotiation is allowed, and indeed the possibility of renegotiation itself is crucial in supporting collusion. The collusive equilibria are obtained in two different settings. First, one round of renegotiation of the incentive schemes is allowed before the product market clears. It is shown that the owners are able to use the first announcement of the incentive schemes to co-ordinate on a collusive equilibrium. In the second setting, production is described as divided into many different sub-periods, in each of which the output produced depends on the manager's incentive scheme. Costly renegotiation is allowed between the production sub-periods, but the effect of a renegotiation becomes observable to the rival with a short delay. The benefits an owner can get by deviating from a collusive allocation in that short period of delay can be so small to be offset by the costs of renegotiation. Hence collusion prevails. The two settings are closely related since in both cases it is the observability of renegotiation that plays a crucial role in supporting the collusive equilibrium.

In section 2 the assumption of observability in delegation games is discussed; in section 3 the basic model is presented; in section 4 the benchmark case equilibrium is determined; in section 5 and 6 the case with one round of renegotiation and with production divided into short sub-periods are analysed; section 7 concludes.

---

[1] A more recent paper presenting a collusive equilibrium in delegation games is Polo-Tedeschi (1997). In their setting collusion is sustained by kinked contracts, which are renegotiation-proof if the side-transfer technology to be used in renegotiations has a dead-weight loss increasing in the size of the transfer.

[2] Like the Competition Authority.

3.2   Observability in delegation games

During the past decade, the literature has witnessed a growing interest in the analysis of games played through agents, building on the seminal work by Schelling (1960). Besides the already cited papers in oligopoly theory, there are many other applications as, for instance, to central banks independence (e.g. Rogoff (1985), Persson-Tabellini (1993), Walsh (1995)), international trade (Gatsios-Karp (1991)) and tax audits (Melumad-Mookherjee (1989)). In these models, at least one player gives up the capability of making decisions concerning an activity influencing his utility and appoints a delegate to make choices in his own place. The equilibrium of the resulting game depends on the delegates' objectives, which may or may not coincide with those of their principals. Standard results for this kind of models show that the principal may benefit by appointing a delegate who takes actions that the principal - were he playing - could not credibly take. In that way the principal may obtain a strategic advantage by including some strategies which would be dominated in the game without delegation within the set of best responses for the new game. This strategic effect can be obtained in two ways: the principal can either exploit his delegate's personal reputation to be of a certain "type" or shape the delegate's preferences through an incentive contract. In this chapter I concentrate on strategic delegation through contracts.

In the absence of distortions due to agency costs, the strategic effect of delegation can be obtained if and only if the other players, be they principals or delegates, when they choose their strategy, can be sure that they know the real incentives of the delegate they are playing with. When delegation is ruled by contracts, this amounts to the perfect observability of them.

Observability requires that

i. the other players are aware of the incentive scheme in full detail;

ii. they are sure that no secret renegotiation can take place.

This can be attained in two ways. First, principals and delegates may have the capability to commit not to renegotiate contracts, once they are announced, even when both parties would be better off by doing so. As mentioned above, this is very frequently assumed in strategic delegation models, although it seems quite a strong requirement. It implies that the parties to a contract can be forced to abide by that even against their consonant will. Implicit agreements to alter the delegate's equilibrium strategy according to the principal's objectives are therefore also ruled out. In most of this chapter I assume that principals and delegates cannot bind themselves in such a strong way and so that contracts are renegotiable. This seems to me a more natural setting. Anyway my analysis is limited to this case and so it is, in this respect, complementary to the case when committing not to renegotiate is an available option.

Another way to have observability, when the parties are allowed to renegotiate if they want to, is to make the renegotiation procedure observable. In fact, it is not the possibility of renegotiation in itself that destroys the commitment value of contracts, but its secrecy. The aim of this chapter is to discuss the consequences of assuming that observability is obtained by making the renegotiation procedure, as well as the main contract, observable. As it will be argued below, the observability of renegotiations may follow from some specific feature of the contract in use, but it turns out that the parties have an incentive to make renegotiations observable, since that allows them to use contracts as a co-ordinating mechanism enabling the principals to credibly signal their collusive intentions and the delegates to monitor the rivals' potential deviations. However, the present analysis can also be motivated on purely theoretical grounds, as an investigation of the consequences of assuming that making renegotiations observable is an available option.

A part of the literature on strategic delegation has concentrated on the role of asymmetric information between the principal and the delegate. Dewatripont (1988), Katz (1991) and Caillaud-Jullien-Picard (1995) show that under asymmetric information strategic pre-commitment can be attained even if contracts are not perfectly observable, when a distortion in the decision to be taken by the delegate is needed for incentive compatibility, provided that the optimum contract between the principal and the delegate is common knowledge.

3.3   The benchmark model

As a benchmark we consider a slight variation of the model of delegation in duopoly by Fershtman-Judd (1987) and Sklivas (1987). The only main difference from their setting is in the utility function of the delegates, which in my model includes a term for the disutility from effort proportional to the quantity produced.

In a symmetric homogeneous-good Cournot duopoly, the firms face the following inverse demand function

$$p = a - b(q_1 + q_2)$$ (3.1)

where p is the price of the product, q_1 and q_2 are the output levels of firm 1 and 2, and the parameter b, the market scale, is a random variable uniformly distributed over the interval $\left[\underline{b}, \overline{b}\right]$. Only a subset of the individuals in the economy, the managers, observe the market scale b before the output levels are chosen and production is carried out. They alone have the skill to correctly monitor the demand and that is why they are delegated the choice of the output level by the owners, who retain residual claims on profits. Apart from the managers' remuneration, the firms' production costs are linear in output and, for simplicity, no fixed costs are considered. Hence firm i's production costs function is the following:

$$C_i = c_i q_i \qquad i=1,2$$ (3.2)

while firm i's revenues and profit, gross of the manager's compensation, are

$$R_i = [a - b(q_1 + q_2)]q_i \qquad i=1,2$$ (3.3)

$$\Pi_i = [a - b(q_1 + q_2)]q_i - c_i q_i \qquad i=1,2$$ (3.4)

The relationship between each owner and his manager is regulated by a contract which makes the managerial wage contingent on the outcome of the firm's activity:

$$W_i = T_i\left[E(b)\right] + \left[w_i \Pi_i + (1 - w_i)R_i\right] = T_i\left[E(b)\right] + \left[R_i - w_i c_i q_i\right]$$
$$i=1,2$$ (3.5)

where W_i is manager i's remuneration and $T_i\left[E(b)\right]$ is a fixed transfer to be determined to satisfy manager i's participation constraint. As in Fershtman-Judd (1987), the choice of the remuneration scheme is split in two parts. First, the owner chooses the parameter w_i in order to provide the manager with the desired incentives. Given the choice of w_i, the lump sum transfer $T_i\left[E(b)\right]$ is set by the owner, contingent on the expected value of the market scale b, in order to keep the manager at his reservation utility in expected terms. The contract is fully characterised by $T_i\left[E(b)\right]$ and w_i. Hereafter, we will denote with $W_i^k\left(.\right)$ a contract between the owner and the manager of firm i, i.e. a pair $\left\{T_i\left[E(b)\right], w_i\right\}$, under "regime" k and w_i^k the associated parameter w_i.

In general the incentive contract can be of many different types, but we limit ourselves to the case of contracts linear in gross profits and revenues. Fershtman-Judd (1987) have shown that linear contracts are a Nash equilibrium choice in the contract- setting game, since they allow to choose any allocation on the rival manager reaction function in the output-setting game, so that no owner would like to individually deviate to a more general contract. Furthermore, they have shown that in the present setting characterised by ex-ante uncertainty linear contracts are preferred to other equilibrium contracts, because facing them the managers will make an optimal use of the information they acquire on b.

Owners maximise profits net of the managers' compensations

$$\pi_i = \Pi_i - W_i = \left[a - b(q_1 + q_2)\right]q_i - c_i q_i - \left[T_i\left[E(b)\right] + \left(R_i - w_i c_i q_i\right)\right]$$
(3.6)

and choose their respective managers' incentive schemes, knowing the managers' preferences and reservation utility. For simplicity we normalise the reservation utility of both managers to be equal to zero, $u_i^0 = 0$.

Both managers have the following additively separable utility function

$$U_i = f_i\left(W_i\right) - e_i\left(q_i\right) \quad i=1,2$$
(3.7)

where $e_i(q_i)$ is the manager's disutility of effort, $f_i'\left(W_i\right) > 0$ and $e_i' > 0$. The manager's disutility of effort is increasing in output, accounting for the fact that the total amount of effort increases in the size of the firm's activity. For simplicity, but without loss of generality, we assume that all the players are risk neutral and the managers' utility function is linear in output, i.e.

$$U_i = W_i - e_i q_i \quad i=1,2$$
(3.7a)

3.4   Non-renegotiable contracts

In this section we determine the equilibrium of the model described above when managerial contracts are simultaneously chosen and non-renegotiable. The analysis follows Fershtman-Judd (1987) apart from the assumption on the disutility of effort and is reported here for the sake of comparison with what follows. In this setting the following assumption holds.

Assumption 3.1. Perfect Commitment Capability. Owners are able to commit themselves not to renegotiate the contracts with their managers even when renegotiation is Pareto improving.

This assumption requires that contracts, once signed, are absolutely binding and cannot be renegotiated even when the parties mutually agree to do so. As noticed above this is quite a strong assumption. However, perfect commitment capability is required for the equilibrium in Fershtman-Judd (1987) to be unique. In the following section it is shown that the same equilibrium can be sustained by assuming that contracts' renegotiations, whenever they take place, are observable. However, under that assumption the equilibrium of Game 3.1 is just one, and indeed the least desirable, of a continuum of equilibria. Under the assumption of perfect commitment capability, the structure of the duopoly delegation game is the following:

Game 3.1 - Strategic delegation with Perfect Commitment Capability

Stage 1. The owners simultaneously choose the incentive schemes for their managers, W_i (.), which become immediately common knowledge to all managers and owners.

Stage 2. Each manager i, after observing b, his own and his rival's incentive schemes, W_1 (.) and W_2 (.), chooses the level of output of his firm. Firms' profits and managers' remunerations are then determined by the market.

The Sub-game Perfect Equilibrium (S.P.E.) of Game 3.1 is determined in the following lemma. We call this the strategic contracting equilibrium and we use superscript s to denote all the equilibrium values which refer to it.

Lemma 3.1. In the S.P.E. of Game 3.1 the incentive schemes for the managers and the levels of output produced are given by:

$$w_1^s = 1 - \frac{a - 3e_1 + 2e_2 - 3c_1 + 2c_2}{5c_1}$$

$$T_1^s = e_1 q_1^s \left[E(b)\right] - \left\{R_1\left[E(b)\right] - w_1^s c_1 q_1^s\left[E(b)\right]\right\},$$

$$w_2^s = 1 - \frac{a - 3e_2 + 2e_1 - 3c_2 + 2c_1}{5c_2}$$

$$T_2^s = e_2 q_2^s \left[E(b)\right] - \left\{R_2\left[E(b)\right] - w_2^s c_2 q_2^s\left[E(b)\right]\right\};$$

$$q_1^s = \frac{2\left(a - 3e_1 + 2e_2 - 3c_1 + 2c_2\right)}{5b}$$

$$q_2^s = \frac{2\left(a - 3e_2 + 2e_1 - 3c_2 + 2c_1\right)}{5b}.$$

Proof. See Appendix 3.1.

It is easy to see that in equilibrium the participation constraints of the delegates bind, so that they are kept at their reservation utility.

Also, if $q_1^s > 0$ and $q_2^s > 0$, then $w_1^s < 1$ and $w_2^s < 1$. This amounts to a move away from profits maximisation in the managers' objective functions, which involves a lower weight on unit costs and so an upward shift of the managers' reaction functions in the output-setting game. Managers behave more aggressively than profit maximisation would require. So, the equilibrium choice of output would not be individually rational if the output-setting game was played directly by the owner, who would renegotiate the contract if he could do it secretly, to go back to a game played with his preferences. In fact, in a game with undetectable renegotiations the owner of one firm could induce his manager to respond optimally to the rival strategic contracting equilibrium choice. However, a secret renegotiation cannot be an available option, otherwise the owner loses his perfect commitment capability and the rival would take advantage of knowing that the owner's delegate has the same preferences as his principal. The strategic contracting equilibrium results, yielding greater output levels, and so lower profits, than in the usual Cournot setting. The equilibrium is inefficient, but the owners are trapped in a Prisoners' Dilemma: they would be better off if both could renounce to their commitment capability, but if only one does renounce, he is worse off.

3.5   One round of renegotiation

In this section we assume that contracts' observability does not follow from perfect commitment capability, but depends on the process of renegotiation being observable to third parties. Observability of renegotiation is sufficient for strategic contracting to be effective as a commitment device; so that perfect commitment capability is not necessary for that purpose. In this setting however the set of equilibrium contracts includes not only the strategic contracting equilibrium analysed in the previous section, but also all the allocations allowing each firm to get at least the profit of the strategic contracting equilibrium, which is used as a threat point in the contract-setting game. We first state the assumption which characterises the setting of this section.

Assumption 3.2. Observability of Renegotiation. The renegotiation of contracts, when it occurs, is observable by any interested third party.

This assumption means that the necessary procedures make renegotiation observable to anyone interested. This seems to be realistic and describes many real life examples, as, for instance, contracts which require collective bargaining or which concern the public sector, where the community on whose behalf the decision is taken has to be informed. Even in the case of owner-manager relationships in private firms the observability assumption seems to be tenable: big companies chief executives' contracts usually have to be ratified by the shareholders' assembly. Furthermore, the fact that all chief executives come from the same social group should facilitate and perhaps give them a reason for monitoring each other. Anyway, it turns out that building a mechanism which makes renegotiation perfectly observable is desirable for the owners, since it allows them to co-ordinate on a collusive outcome.

We allow only one round of renegotiation to take place. At an intermediate stage, in between the signing of the managerial contracts and production, either one owner-manager couple or both can agree to renegotiate or, alternatively, one of the managers or both can force a renegotiation on their counterpart by threatening to give up the job. In any of these cases, the intentions to renegotiate are observed by the rival firm and both managerial contracts are simultaneously renegotiated. Otherwise, contracts remain unchanged. It might be clarifying to notice, already at this stage, that once renegotiation takes place in one firm the contract selected in the rival firm may no longer be an equilibrium, since the participation constraint of the manager gets violated. This is typically the case when the renegotiating owner tries to make an output-increasing renegotiation. This structure for the renegotiation process can be thought as a reduced form for a sequence of observable renegotiations and counter-renegotiations by the two firms, which may take place before the output-setting game is started. The structure of the game with renegotiation is slightly modified from Game 3.1 to include a further stage as follows.

Game 3.2 - Delegation with One Round of Renegotiation

Stage 1. The owners simultaneously choose the incentive schemes for their managers, W_i (.), which become common knowledge to all managers and owners.

Stage 2. After observing the W_1 (.) and W_2 (.) selected at stage 1, managers and owners state their intentions to renegotiate their contracts or to abide by them. If either manager or both want to renegotiate, the incentive schemes are simultaneously renegotiated in both firms. If either owner or both want to renegotiate and at least one manager accepts to do so, the incentive schemes are simultaneously renegotiated. Otherwise, the contracts remain unchanged.

Stage 3. Each manager i, after observing b, given the possibly renegotiated incentive schemes, chooses the level of output of his firm, which becomes observable to his owner. Firms' profits and managers' remuneration are determined by the market.

We confine our attention only to symmetric equilibria.

It is easy to see that if renegotiation takes place, the choice of a new contract to replace the old one is equivalent to the choice of the contract in stage 1 of Game 3.1. Therefore, whenever renegotiation takes place, the equilibrium of Game 3.2 is the strategic contracting equilibrium we have calculated for Game 3.1. The set of equilibria of Game 3.2 may however include also further renegotiation-proof equilibria. In order to determine the set of renegotiation-proof equilibria, it is useful to introduce the following definition of mutual consistency of the incentive schemes.

Definition 3.1 - Mutually Consistent Contracts. A pair of contracts $\left\{W_1(.), W_2(.)\right\}$ are mutually consistent, if, once implemented, they allow both managers to get at least their reservation utility, i.e., $U_1\left[W_1(.), W_2(.)\right] \geq u_1^0 = 0$ and $U_2\left[W_1(.), W_2(.)\right] \geq u_2^0 = 0$.[3]

If a pair of non-mutually consistent incentive schemes are chosen, one of the managers or both would call for a renegotiation. If the incentive schemes are mutually consistent, then both managers receive their reservation utility and so have no incentive to call for a renegotiation, given that, as we have seen, a renegotiation necessarily leads them to get their reservation utility. Mutual consistency is therefore a necessary condition for no renegotiation in equilibrium.

Lemma 3.2. A pair of contracts are renegotiation-proof only if they are mutually consistent.

Within the set of mutually consistent contracts we distinguish a sub-set of optimal mutually consistent contracts which give to the managers exactly their reservation utility.

Definition 3.2 - Optimal Mutually Consistent Contracts. A pair of contracts are optimal mutually consistent, if they are mutually consistent and allow the managers to get just their reservation utility, i.e. $U_1\left[W_1(.), W_2(.)\right] = u_1^0 = 0$ and $U_2\left[W_1(.), W_2(.)\right] = u_2^0 = 0$.

The set of optimal mutually consistent contracts contains both contracts which are better and contracts which are worse for the owners than the equilibrium contracts of Game 3.1. Let W^{s+} be the set of optimal mutually consistent contracts leading both firms to level of output higher than q_i^s, the strategic contracting equilibrium output. As quantities are

---

[3] The mutual consistency requirement is obviously satisfied by the equilibrium of Game 3.1, since the simultaneous maximisation of the owners' objective functions satisfy the individual rationality constraints of their managers.

strategic substitutes, any pair of contracts $W \in W^{s+}$ is worse for the owners than the strategic contracting equilibrium, because it implies lower gross profits and higher remuneration to pay for the increased effort of the managers. Therefore, in equilibrium the owners will call for a renegotiation if $W \in W^{s+}$.

On the other hand, let W^{s-} be the set of optimal mutually consistent contracts leading both firms to produce less than in the strategic contracting case and more or equal to half the joint profit maximising output. Any $W \in W^{s-}$ is better for the owners than the strategic contracting equilibrium, since both firms' gross profits increase as their outputs are reduced until the joint profit maximising level is reached, whereas lower level of output imply lower wages to be paid to managers. Therefore, we can state the following lemma.

Lemma 3.3. The subset W^{s-} of optimal mutually consistent contracts is renegotiation-proof.

Proof. Any pair of contracts belonging to W^{s-} is preferred by the owners to the strategic contracting equilibrium which results from a renegotiation and provide the managers with their reservation utilities. Therefore, managers and owners will not call for a renegotiation in equilibrium. (Q.E.D.)

Now we are ready to prove the following proposition.

Proposition 3.4. In a duopoly game with delegation and one round of perfectly observable renegotiation, a symmetric pair of linear contracts W^r is an equilibrium if and only if $W^r \in W^{s-}$.

Proof. For any pair of incentive schemes $\{W_1^r(.), W_2^r(.)\} \in W^{s-}$ it is true that $E\{\pi_i \left[W_1^r(.), W_2^r(.) \right]\} \geq E\{\pi_i \left[W_1^s(.), W_2^s(.) \right]\}$ for $i=1,2$. Let q_1^r and q_2^r be the Nash equilibrium levels of output of the Cournot game where managers have incentive schemes $\{W_1^r(.), W_2^r(.)\}$. Proposition 3.4 says that the following is a sub-game perfect equilibrium of Game 3.2:

$$\{W_1^r(.), W_2^r(.)\};$$

no renegotiation;

$$q_1^r, q_2^r.$$

As above, the game is solved starting from the last stage and moving backward.

At stage 3, if the selected incentive schemes are $W_1^r(.)$ and $W_2^r(.)$, the managers, by definition, choose q_1^r and q_2^r. They are the Nash equilibrium of the Cournot game where managers have incentive schemes $W_1^r(.)$ and $W_2^r(.)$. For any other pair of mutually consistent remuneration schemes, including $W_1^s(.)$ and $W_2^s(.)$, the equilibrium output levels will be the Cournot-Nash equilibrium of the output setting game resulting from the managers having those remuneration schemes. Any pair of incentive schemes not mutually consistent will be renegotiated at stage 2. Hence, no manager will confront the choice of output with a remuneration scheme not allowing him to get at least his reservation utility in expected terms.

At stage 2 neither manager calls for a renegotiation if the pair of incentive schemes chosen by the owners is mutually consistent, but they choose to renegotiate otherwise. If either manager chooses to renegotiate, the incentive schemes are simultaneously renegotiated, the game becomes equal to Game 3.1 and $W_1^s(.)$ and $W_2^s(.)$ are selected. Owner i calls for a renegotiation if the expected profit net of his manager's remuneration for the pair of contracts selected at stage 1 is smaller than the net expected profit in the strategic contracting equilibrium, i.e. if $E\left\{\pi_i\left[W_1(.),W_2(.)\right]\right\} < E\left\{\pi_i\left[W_1^s(.),W_2^s(.)\right]\right\}$. Hence, if the pair of contracts selected at stage 1 is $\left\{W_1(.),W_2(.)\right\} \in W^{s+}$, the owners will call for a renegotiation. Given that the pair of contracts selected at stage 1 is optimal mutually consistent, the managers agree to renegotiate, because they are already at their reservation utility and so are indifferent between renegotiating and confirming the contracts. If the pair of contracts selected at stage 1 are mutually consistent, but not optimal mutually consistent while both $U_1\left[W_1(.),W_2(.)\right] > u_1^0$ and $U_2\left[W_1(.),W_2(.)\right] > u_2^0$ hold, the managers will not renegotiate. Otherwise, at least one manager agrees to start a renegotiation.

At stage 1 the owners select a pair of optimal mutually consistent contracts $\left\{W_1^r(.),W_2^r(.)\right\} \in W^{s-}$. A pair of non-mutually consistent contracts will not be selected, because otherwise at least one manager will call for a renegotiation at stage 2 and the equilibrium contracts will be $\left\{W_1^s(.),W_2^s(.)\right\}$, which are strictly worse than $\left\{W_1^r(.),W_2^r(.)\right\}$ for the owners.

Non-optimal mutually consistent contracts will not be selected, because the owners can always choose a pair of contracts allowing them to give their managers the same incentives at a lower cost by adjusting T_i. Furthermore, an owner will not select a contract which gives more than his reservation utility to the manager, because the manager would refuse to renegotiate that contract if the owner wanted to do so.

An optimal mutually consistent pair of contracts $\left\{W_1(.),W_2(.)\right\}\in W^{s+}$ will not be selected because they will be renegotiated at stage 2 to get $\left\{W_1^s(.),W_2^s(.)\right\}$, which are preferred by the owners while keeping the managers at their reservation utility.

Finally, any $\left\{W_1^r(.),W_2^r(.)\right\}\in W^{s-}$ is an equilibrium, because no owner can profitably deviate from it by selecting any other contract at stage 1, since any profitable deviation instigates a renegotiation. To be profitable, a deviation must involve an increase in the level of output, since $q_i^r < q_i^s$ implies $w_i^r > w_i^s$, while w_i^s is the Nash equilibrium of the contract-setting game without renegotiation and the w_i are strategic substitutes. A deviation implying an increase in the output of the deviating firm reduces the price of the product and so the rival firm's profit. A reduction in the rival firm's profit violates the individual rationality constraint of the manager, who would then force a renegotiation. (Q.E.D.)

The mutual consistency requirement implies that each owner chooses the incentive scheme taking both his own and his rival manager's individual rationality constraints into account. If either owner deviates from a given pair of optimal mutually consistent incentive schemes trying to increase his profits, his rival's manager individual rationality constraint gets violated, and so the contract in use in the rival firm is no longer an equilibrium. Renegotiation takes place and the game transforms into the previously discussed Game 3.1, whose equilibrium is the strategic contracting equilibrium $\left\{W_1^s(.),W_2^s(.)\right\}$. Therefore, mutually consistent pairs of incentive schemes - preferred by both owners to the strategic allocation but not attainable as a Nash equilibria of the game without renegotiation - can be implemented, because the threat of deviation is made void by the possibility of renegotiation. The strategic contracting equilibrium is used as a threat point to sustain better allocations.

As we have just seen, the delegation game with renegotiation has a continuum of equilibria $\{W_1^r(.),W_2^r(.)\}\in W^{s-}$. So we face an equilibrium selection problem. If the incentive schemes selected by the owners are not mutually consistent, one of the managers will expect not to get his reservation utility and ask for renegotiation, going back to the strategic contracting equilibrium, the only stable equilibrium of the game. Nonetheless, the equilibrium selection problem may be tackled by using a focal point argument. As it is well known, a linear Cournot duopoly game has a unique Pareto efficient symmetric allocation: the one corresponding to the joint profit maximising outputs. Choosing that allocation, within a continuum of equilibria, seems quite an obvious way to play Game 3.2. Therefore we can state the following proposition.

Proposition 3.5. Let $\{W_1^c(.),W_2^c(.)\}$ be the pair of optimal mutually consistent linear incentive schemes implementing the output levels corresponding to joint profit maximisation net of the managers' remuneration. The focal point sub-game perfect equilibrium of a duopoly model with delegation and perfectly observable renegotiation is the following

$$\{W_1^c(.),W_2^c(.)\};$$

no renegotiation;

$$q_1^c,q_2^c.$$

The contract and the output levels corresponding to joint profit maximisation can be easily calculated as shown in Appendix 3.2, they are:

$$w_1^c = w_2^c = w^c = \frac{a-e+3c}{4c} = 1+\frac{a-e-c}{4c}, \tag{3.8}$$

$$T_1^c = T_2^c = T^c = eq^c\left[E(b)\right] - \left\{R\left[E(b)\right] - w^c cq^c\left[E(b)\right]\right\}; \tag{3.9}$$

$$q_1^c = q_2^c = q^c = \frac{(a-e-c)}{4b}. \tag{3.10}$$

We notice that if in equilibrium $q^c > 0$, then $w^c > 1$. This implies that in any equilibrium when firms find it worth producing, the weight on unit costs in the managers' objective is more than for profit maximisation, so that managers' reaction functions are shifted downward. Managers are more cautious than profit maximisation would require.

A final remark on the choice of linear managerial contracts among all the possible kind of contracts available is due. As we noticed above, the choice of linear contracts is one of the many possible Nash equilibria in the game without renegotiation. When renegotiation is considered, as in Game 3.2, linear contracts are still a Nash equilibrium choice of contracts for the same reasons as above. However, as it has been shown, in this case they also allow the attainment of the best symmetric allocation in the output-setting game, i.e., joint profit maximisation. Therefore, they are an optimal choice in the contract setting game.

3.6   Delayed observability and renegotiation costs

In this section we relax the assumption that a contract's renegotiation carried out by one firm becomes immediately observable to the rival manager. We assume that the renegotiation becomes observable after a short delay, during which a firm can take advantage of a change of strategy. After that short interval however the rival manager notices that a renegotiation has taken place, so that his firm can react by renegotiating as well. The size of the benefit a firm can get by renegotiating the managerial contract and taking its rival by surprise is limited by the fact that production requires time. In standard models of oligopoly the choice of output is usually described as a timeless decision, as if the production activity could be carried out instantaneously. [4] However, production takes time and the output decision of the firm can be modified while the production activity is taking place. This can be exploited by the firms to collude.

We show that even in this setting, the set of equilibrium pairs of incentive contracts includes, among many others, the pair of contracts corresponding to joint profit maximisation, provided that the delay

---

[4] Saloner (1987), Basu (1990) and Pal (1991) are noticeable exceptions.

between a renegotiation and its detection by the rival firm is not too long and there are positive, although not necessarily large, renegotiation costs.[5]

As above we consider a symmetric homogeneous-good Cournot duopoly.

Production for a given year takes place in a finite number of production sub-periods $\frac{T}{2}$, which we call days; at the end of each day the output produced in that day is sold.

Between the production sub-periods there are $\frac{T}{2}$ sub-periods, which we call nights, in which renegotiation of managerial contracts can take place.

Renegotiation is costly. Each round of renegotiation imposes a cost r to be borne by the owner of the firm.

If renegotiation takes place, it becomes observable to the other firm's manager one sub-period later, i.e. at the beginning of the following production sub-period.

Dynamic contracts specifying different incentives for the manager in different production sub-periods are ruled out because their complexity would make them impossible to enforce by a third party.

We assume that the manager's effort is quadratic in output per sub-period, so that the optimum output per sub-period is limited by the manager's capability to cope. Otherwise we maintain that unit cost is constant. Therefore, the managers' utility function in a given period (day plus night) will be

$$U_i = W_i - q_i^2 \tag{3.11}$$

The two firms face a linear inverse demand function in each sub-period

$$p = a - b(q_1 + q_2). \tag{3.12}$$

---

[5] In a somewhat related setting McCutcheon (1997) has recently discussed the role of renegotiation costs in supporting tacit collusion. For example the Sherman Act forbids and sanctions meetings to discuss prices. This may help firms to sustain collusive agreements by preventing them from renegotiating away market place punishments to cheaters, which may not be time consistent.

For simplicity we assume that all the parameters of the demand function are known to everybody.

In all other respects the model is the same as above, and again we limit our attention to consider only linear contracts, which can be used to implement the symmetric Pareto-efficient allocation. In this new setting the structure of the duopolistic game becomes the following:

Game 3.3 - Delegation with delayed observability and costly renegotiation

Stage 0. The owners simultaneously choose the incentive schemes for their managers W_i $(.)$, and announce them publicly.

Odd Stages. Having observed the rival manager's incentive scheme as it was at the end of the previous stage, the manager can force a renegotiation, while the owner can propose it to his manager. If the manager agrees, renegotiation takes place. If the contract is renegotiated, the owner bears a renegotiation cost r. If no renegotiation occurs, contracts W_1 $(.)$ and W_2 $(.)$ carry over to the next period.[6]

Even Stages. After observing his and the rival manager's incentive schemes as they are at the beginning of the present sub-period t, W_1 (t) and W_2 (t), the managers choose the level of output for t. At the end of the sub-period the quantities are sold and profit and remuneration for that sub-period are determined.

We notice that after stage 0 the game just described is a repeated game of which each stage is composed of a contract renegotiation sub-period and an output setting sub-period. In each even stage manager i chooses q_i to maximise the following with respect to q_i:

$$U_i = T_i\left(b\right) + \left[a - b\left(q_1 + q_2\right)\right]q_i - w_i c_i q_i - q_i^2 \qquad (3.13)$$

The output levels as functions of the incentive contracts, and so of the w's, will then be:

$$q_1' = \frac{2a + ab - 2c_1 w_1 - 2bc_1 w_1 + bc_2 w_2}{4 + 8b + 3b^2} \qquad (3.14)$$

---

[6] Hence we are considering a sort of inertia super-game as that in Chakrabarti (1990).

$$q_2' = \frac{2a + ab - 2c_2w_2 - 2bc_2w_2 + bc_1w_1}{4 + 8b + 3b^2}.$$

$$(3.15)$$

Before analysing the equilibrium of Game 3.3, we need to state some definitions.

Definition 3.3 - Stackelberg Leader Contract. A Stackelberg leader contract for firm i, W_i^{sl}, is the contract maximising the stage profit of firm i, given that the contract of firm j is selected as a best reply to the contract of firm i.

Definition 3.4 - Stackelberg Follower Contract. A Stackelberg follower contract for firm i, W_i^{sf}, is the contract maximising the stage profit of firm i, given that the contract of firm j is a Stackelberg leader contract.

In our setting a Stackelberg leader contract for firm 1 can be selected in the following way. We substitute (3.14) and (3.15) into the net profit function for firm 2; then we maximise it with respect to w_2 for a given w_1 to get

$$w_2^{sf} = \frac{-2ab^2 - ab^3 + 8c_2 + 24bc_2 + 22b^2c_2 + 6b^3c_2 - b^3c_1w_1}{\left(8 + 24b + 20b^2 + 4b^3\right)c_2}$$

$$(3.16)$$

Then we substitute w_2^{sf} back into the net profit function for firm 1 and maximise with respect to w_1 to get

$$w_1^{sl} = \frac{a\left(-4b^2 - 6b^3 - b^4\right) + c_1\left(16 + 64b + 84b^2 + 40b^3 + 6b^4\right) - c_2\left(2b^3 + 2b^4\right)}{\left(16 + 64b + 80b^2 + 32b^3 + 3b^4\right)c_1}$$

$$(3.17)$$

Both for the Stackelberg leader and the Stackelberg follower contract the lump-sum transfers T_i are selected to keep the managers at their reservation utilities. The Stackelberg leader stage profit net of the manager's remuneration will be

$$\pi_i\left(W_i^{sl},W_j^{sf}\right)=\frac{\left(4a+6ab+ab^2-4c_1-8bc_1-3b^2c_1+2bc_2+2b^2c_2\right)^2}{\left(64+320b+576b^2+448b^3+140b^4+12b^5\right)}$$

(3.18)

Definition 3.5 - Best Reply Contract. A best reply contract for firm i, $W_i^{br}\left(W_j\right)$, is the contract maximising firm i's net profit for a given contract of firm j.

Again, the lump-sum transfer T_i is selected in order to keep the manager at his reservation utility. We are now ready to prove the following proposition.

Proposition 3.6. Any pair of strategies implying a choice of a pair of optimal mutually consistent contracts $\left(W_i^*,W_j^*\right)$ at stage 0, where $\pi_i\left(W_i^*,W_j^*\right)\geq\pi_i\left(W_i^{sl},W_j^{sf}\right)$ and $\pi_i\left(W_i^{br}\left(W_j^*\right),W_j^*\right)-\pi_i\left(W_i^*,W_j^*\right)-r\leq0$ for $i=1,2;i\neq j$, and no renegotiation at any stage, is a sub-game perfect equilibrium of Game 3.3.

Proof. Given $\pi_i\left(W_i^{br}\left(W_j^*\right),W_j^*\right)-\pi_i\left(W_i^*,W_j^*\right)-r\leq0$ and optimum mutual consistency of incentive contracts, at stage T-1, if the contracts are $\left(W_i^*,W_j^*\right)$, neither the owners nor the managers have incentives to renegotiate. For the same reason there is no short-term gain from a best-reply deviation at any previous stage of the game.

Given that any profitable deviation from W_i^* will make the rival firm renegotiate, since the manager's participation constraint would be no longer satisfied,[7] all the available deviations from $\left(W_i^*,W_j^*\right)$ are worse for owner i than to choose a Stackelberg leader contract at stage 0 and renounce to his firm capability to renegotiate.[8] Given $\pi_i\left(W_i^*,W_j^*\right)\geq\pi_i\left(W_i^{sl},W_j^{sf}\right)$, it is optimum for both owners not to

---

[7] The same argument on profitable deviation violating the rival manager's participation constraint used in the Proof of Proposition 3.4 applies here.
[8] Renouncing to the capability to renegotiate is not allowed within the game, but the argument used in the proof applies to any deviation worse than that for the owner.

deviate from $\left(W_i^*, W_j^*\right)$. Therefore, $\left(W_i^*, W_j^*\right)$ is a sub-game perfect equilibrium of game 3.3. (Q.E.D)

Corollary 3.7. If either of the following holds

$$c_1 = c_2 < a$$

$$c_i < \frac{16a + 60ab + 72ab^2 + 29ab^3 + 3ab^4 + 4bc_j + 12b^2c_j + 11b^3c_j + 3b^4c_j}{16 + 64b + 84b^2 + 40b^3 + 6b^4}$$

$$- \frac{(1+b)\sqrt{\left(128 + 768b + 1712b^2 + 1728b^3 + 776b^4 + 144b^5 + 9b^6\right)}\left(a - c_j\right)}{16 + 64b + 84b^2 + 40b^3 + 6b^4}$$

and $\quad r \geq \dfrac{b^2\left(-2a - 3ab - bc_1 - b^2c_1 + 2c_2 + 4bc_2 + b^2c_2\right)^2}{32\left(1 + 2b\right)^2\left(2 + 6b + 5b^2 + b^3\right)}$, the

pair of contracts which maximise joint profit, $\left(W_i^{cc}, W_j^{cc}\right)$, is a sub-game perfect equilibrium of Game 3.3.

Proof. See Appendix 3.1.

As the delay by which the renegotiation of one firm's contract is detected by the rival decreases, the length of the production sub-periods is shortened, so that the single sub-period's profit gets smaller. Hence, we would expect that the more quickly renegotiation is observable, the smaller is the incentive to deviate, the more is likely that collusion prevails. This can be easily shown by modelling a reduction in the length of sub-periods in the following way.

We add a parameter λ to the manager objective function (3.13) to get

$$U_i = T_i(b) + \left[a - \lambda b(q_1 + q_2)\right]q_i - w_i c_i q_i - \lambda q_i^2 \qquad (3.13a)$$

When sub-periods get shorter, in each of them the market size reduces and more effort is needed to produce the same quantity. Hence, a reduction in the delay corresponds to an increase in λ.

Lemma 3.8. When λ increases the incentive to deviate from collusion decreases.

Proof. By taking λ into account it is easy to show that the incentive to deviate becomes:

$$\frac{b^2\left(-2a-3ab-bc_1-b^2c_1+2c_2+4bc_2+b^2c_2\right)^2}{32\left(1+2b\right)^2\left(2+6b+5b^2+b^3\right)\lambda}-r \quad (3.19)$$

which becomes smaller as λ increases. (Q.E.D.)

3.7 Conclusions

This chapter is focused on the role of delegation contracts as a co-ordination device. Through the example of firms competing in a duopolistic market, it is shown that agents playing games characterised by non-efficient equilibria may find it profitable to play through delegates in order to reach cooperative allocations.

In two different but closely related settings, it has been shown that the observability of the incentive contracts, together with the possibility of renegotiating them, allow duopolistic firms to support implicit collusive agreements.

If the renegotiation which takes place in a firm can be immediately detected and reacted against by the rival, the equilibrium which results from renegotiation will be used as a threat to sustain collusion. If renegotiation only becomes observable to rivals with a delay, but it is costly, then, if the delay is short enough, renegotiation costs offset the gains of deviating from collusion. The incentive to deviate is also shown to decrease as the delay by which renegotiation becomes observable to the rival shrinks.

The incentive schemes used to implement collusion in this chapter all imply that managers' remuneration is positively related to profits. Hence, they cannot be easily detected as an anti-competitive practice. The results obtained provide two other examples of sustainable collusive equilibria. They seem to reinforce the argument that collusion may be the prevailing industries' configuration in real world oligopolies and, more generally, the claim for public intervention to discipline markets.

Appendix 3.1 - Proofs of Lemma 3.1 and of Corollary 3.7

Proof of Lemma 3.1. Game 3.1 is solved by applying backward induction. At stage two, both managers maximise the difference between their remuneration and disutility of effort:

$$\underset{q_i}{Max} \quad U_i = T_i + R_i - w_i c_i q_i - e_i q_i \qquad\qquad i = 1,2 \quad i \neq j$$

$$(3.A1)$$

Therefore, the optimum choice of q_i will be a function of both the parameters w_i in the incentive schemes:

$$q_i = \frac{\left(a - 2e_i + e_j - 2c_i w_i + c_j w_j\right)}{3b} \qquad\qquad (3.A2)$$

At stage one both owners take the consequences of their choices of w on their managers decisions into account and maximise their expected net profits:

$$\underset{w_i}{Max\, E(\pi_i)} = \int_{\underline{b}}^{\overline{b}} \left\{ \left[a - \left(\frac{\left(a-2e_i+e_j-2c_i w_i +c_j w_j\right)}{3} + \frac{\left(a-2e_j+e_i-2c_j w_j +c_i w_i\right)}{3} \right) \right] \right.$$

$$\left. \left(\frac{\left(a-2e_i+e_j-2c_i w_i +c_j w_j\right)}{3b} \right) - \left(e_i +c_i\right)\frac{\left(a-2e_i+e_j-2c_i w_i +c_j w_j\right)}{3b} \right\} f(b) db$$

$$i = 1,2 \quad i \neq j \qquad\qquad (3.A3)$$

where $f(b)$ is the density function for b and in the objective function we have already substituted the individual rationality constraint

$$-\int_{\underline{b}}^{\overline{b}} e_i \frac{\left(a - 2e_i + e_j - 2c_i w_i + c_j w_j\right)}{3b} f(b)\, db - E[T_i(b) + (R_i - w_i c_i q_i)] \geq 0$$

$$(3.A3a)$$

which binds in equilibrium.[9]

We notice that, given managers' and owners' risk neutrality the maximand for the owners' problem can be written as a function of the expected value of $\frac{1}{b}$, that we denote by $\frac{1}{\hat{b}}$. Hence, (3.A3) becomes

$$\underset{w_i}{Max}\, E(\pi_i) = \left[a - \left(\frac{\left(a-2e_i +e_j -2c_i w_i +c_j w_j\right)}{3} + \frac{\left(a-2e_j +e_i -2c_j w_j +c_i w_i\right)}{3} \right) \right]$$

$$\left(\frac{\left(a-2e_i +e_j -2c_i w_i +c_j w_j\right)}{\hat{b}} \right) - \left(e_i +c_i\right) \frac{\left(a-2e_i +e_j -2c_i w_i +c_j w_j\right)}{\hat{b}}$$

$$i = 1,2 \quad i \neq j \tag{3.A3b}$$

From the simultaneous solution of the two maximisation problems in (3.A3b), for firm 1 and 2, we obtain

$$w_1^s = 1 - \frac{a-3e_1 +2e_2 -3c_1 +2c_2}{5c_1} \tag{3.A4a}$$

$$w_2^s = 1 - \frac{a-3e_2 +2e_1 -3c_2 +2c_1}{5c_2}. \tag{3.A4b}$$

Finally, by substituting w_1^s and w_2^s in equation (3.A2), we get

$$q_1^s = \frac{2\left(a-3e_1 +2e_2 -3c_1 +2c_2\right)}{5b} \tag{3.A5a}$$

$$q_2^s = \frac{2\left(a-3e_2 +2e_1 -3c_2 +2c_1\right)}{5b}. \tag{3.A5b}$$

(Q.E.D.)

---

[9] The relationships between managers and owners are characterised by an informational asymmetry. However, as we have seen, this does not give rise to opportunistic behaviour of the managers, since output and the market size are revealed to the owners ex-post. Therefore, there is no need for an incentive compatibility constraint in the owner maximisation problem; only the individual rationality constraint holds and the manager is kept at his reservation utility.

Proof of Corollary 3.7. It is easy to show that the pair of joint profit maximising contract satisfies $\pi_i \left(W_i^{cc}, W_j^{cc} \right) \geq \pi_i \left(W_i^{sl}, W_j^{sf} \right)$.

The owners maximise joint profit by selecting the incentive contracts in the following way. We substitute (3.14) and (3.15) in the expression for joint profit to obtain:

$$\pi_1 + \pi_2 = \left\{ a - b\left[q_1'(.) + q_2'(.) \right] \right\} \left[q_1'(.) + q_2'(.) \right] - c_1 q_1'(.) - c_2 q_2'(.) - \left[q_1'(.) \right]^2 - \left[q_2'(.) \right]^2$$
$$(3.A6)$$

$(3.A6)$ is then maximised with respect to w_1 and w_2, to get

$$w_1^{cc} = \frac{ab - bc_2 - b^2 c_2 + 2c_1 + 4bc_1 + b^2 c_1}{2c_1 + 4bc_1}$$
$$(3.A7a)$$

$$w_2^{cc} = \frac{ab - bc_1 - b^2 c_1 + 2c_2 + 4bc_2 + b^2 c_2}{2c_2 + 4bc_2}$$
$$(3.A7b)$$

The corresponding net profit for firm 1 and 2 are:

$$\pi_1 \left(W_1^{cc}, W_2^{cc} \right) = \frac{(a - c_1)(a - c_1 - bc_1 + bc_2)}{4 + 8b}$$
$$(3.A8a)$$

$$\pi_2 \left(W_2^{cc}, W_1^{cc} \right) = \frac{(a - c_2)(a - c_2 - bc_2 + bc_1)}{4 + 8b}$$
$$(3.A8b)$$

The difference between the profit from collusion and the Stackelberg leader profit for firm 1 is

$$\pi_1 \left(W_1^{cc}, W_2^{cc} \right) - \pi_1 \left(W_1^{sl}, W_2^{sf} \right) = \frac{(a - c_1)(a - c_1 - bc_1 + bc_2)}{4 + 8b} -$$

$$- \frac{\left(4a + 6ab + ab^2 - 4c_1 - 8bc_1 - 3b^2 c_1 + 2bc_2 + 2b^2 c_2 \right)^2}{\left(64 + 320b + 576b^2 + 448b^3 + 140b^4 + 12b^5 \right)}$$

$$(3.A9)$$

It is easy to see that this is always positive for $c_1 = c_2 < a$ or whenever the following is satisfied

$$c_1 < \frac{16a+60ab+72ab^2 +29ab^3 +3ab^4 +4bc_2 +12b^2c_2 +11b^3c_2 +3b^4c_2}{16+64b+84b^2 +40b^3 +6b^4}$$

$$\frac{(1+b)\sqrt{(128+768b+1712b^2 +1728b^3 +776b^4 +144b^5 +9b^6)}(a-c_2)}{16+64b+84b^2 +40b^3 +6b^4}$$

$$(3.A10)$$

When (3.A9) is positive and contracts are mutually consistent, no renegotiation will occur at any sub-period between 1 and T-2. At T-1, the best reply net profit for firm 1, if its owner and manager renegotiate to deviate from a collusive pair of contracts, is

$$\pi_1\left(W_1^{br}\left(W_2^{cc}\right),W_2^{cc}\right)=\frac{\left[a\left(4+10b+5b^2\right)-c_1\left(4+12b+9b^2 +b^3\right)+c_2\left(2b+4b^2 +b^3\right)\right]^2}{32\left(1+b\right)\left(1+2b\right)^2\left(2+4b+b^2\right)}$$

$$(3.A11)$$

The incentive to deviate at stage T-1 is the difference between (3.A11) and the sum of (3.A8a) plus r. Therefore, at stage T-1, firm 1's contract is not renegotiated to deviate from collusion if

$$r \geq \pi_1\left(W_1^{br}\left(W_2^{cc}\right),W_2^{cc}\right)-\pi_1^{cc}\left(W_1^{cc},W_2^{cc}\right)=$$

$$=\frac{b^2\left(-2a-3ab-bc_1 -b^2c_1 +2c_2 +4bc_2 +b^2c_2\right)^2}{32\left(1+2b\right)^2\left(2+6b+5b^2 +b^3\right)} \qquad (3.A12)$$

(Q.E.D.)

Appendix 3.2 - The computation of a collusive equilibrium

The equilibrium contracts and output in the collusive equilibrium are easily calculated as follows. At stage 3 the managers choose the optimum levels of output exactly as in the strategic case. Hence, the choice of manager i will be as in equation (3.A2):

$$q_i = \frac{\left(a - 2e_i + e_j - 2c_i w_i + c_j w_j\right)}{3b} \qquad i, j = 1,2 \quad i \neq j \qquad (3.A2)$$

In the perfectly symmetric case, (3.A2) reduces to:

$$q_i = \frac{\left(a - e - cw\right)}{3b} \qquad\qquad (3.A13)$$

Given these decision rules, the owners choose the incentive schemes in order to make the sum of q_1 and q_2 equal to the joint profits maximising output Q^c:

$$q_1^c = q_2^c = \frac{Q^c}{2} \qquad\qquad (3.A14)$$

The joint profit maximising output is simply determined by solving the following:

$$\underset{Q}{Max} \ (a - bQ)Q - (e + c)Q \qquad\qquad (3.A15)$$

Hence,

$$Q^c = \frac{\left(a - e - c\right)}{2b} \qquad\qquad (3.A16)$$

while

$$q_1^c = q_2^c = q^c = \frac{\left(a - e - c\right)}{4b} \qquad\qquad (3.A17)$$

Substituting (3.A17) in (3.A13) we get:

$$\frac{\left(a - e - cw\right)}{3b} = \frac{\left(a - e - c\right)}{4b} \qquad\qquad (3.A18)$$

which allows us to calculate the parameter w of the collusive incentive scheme:

$$w_1^c = w_2^c = w^c = \frac{a-e+3c}{4c} = 1 + \frac{a-e-c}{4c} \qquad (3.A19)$$

Chapter 4 - Strategic delegation in the trade union

4.1 Introduction [o]

After having seen strategic delegation at work within firms, in this chapter we study how it may affect the organisation and the activity of the trade union.

The strategic use of delegation is not a possibility reserved only for firms. Any organisation may try to do the same in order to gain a strategic advantage. In particular, unions can try to take advantage of this strategic device in the bargaining relationship with firms. We explore this possibility by considering the effect on the bargaining outcome of the delegation of decisional power from union's members to a professional leader.

We draw a parallel between the firm and the Trade Union and introduce a representation of the union as an incomplete contract with delegation of authority. By giving up the possibility of a collective management of the workers interests, the union offsets the problem of time inconsistency of threats during the bargaining process. A professional leader can credibly choose the arshest threats of industrial actions, which would not be implemented if workers were in control because of their costs in terms of lost earnings.

[o] This chapter is the only section of this book that does not belong to my Ph.D. Thesis. Its homogeneity with the topic of the thesis suggested me to include it here to complete the scope of the analysis proposed. A financial support of MURST ex-40% Research Programme on "Cambiamento strutturale, cambiamento istituzionale e dinamica economica" is gratefully acknowledged

In section 2 we introduce the representation of unions as a political institution characterised by delegated authority; in section 3 we present a model of wage and employment determination with threats of industrial actions, which is a simple version of Moene (1988); in section 4 we analyse the equilibrium for the case when the leader who bargain on the union' behalf is one of the workers; while section 5 contains the case of a professional leader. Section 6 concludes.

4.2   The nature of the trade union: co-ordination costs and the delegation of authority

The debate on the nature of the Trade Union has its origins in the contributions of Dunlop (1944) and Ross (1948). The former sees the Trade Union as the mere sum of the members' wills and addresses the problem of an analytical representation of that sum of wills in a well-defined objective function. Ross, on the other hand, prefers to highlight the Trade Union nature as a political institution. The Trade Union "as an organisation, is not identical with its members, as individuals." (Ross, 1948, p.23, quoted by Pemberton, 1988), but it has its own goals. This view has been disregarded for a long time in the literature; most authors have concentrated their attention on a simple and precise definition of the Union's objective function. Only recently Dunlop's contribution has been revisited by Pemberton (1988), who suggests distinguishing within the Union between subjects with potentially different objectives, such as the *membership* and the *leadership*. This draws a parallel with the distinction between ownership and control in the theory of the firm.

Following this line of thought, we consider the Trade Union as a political institution with delegated authority. Decisions on the bargaining process are not taken through direct consultation of all members, but they are delegated to a leader. So, the union's will is something different from the one of the members and can at least partially misrepresent the members' preferences.

In order to explain the nature of the Trade Union and the emergence of strategic delegation within it, we build a parallel with the literature on the role of transaction costs in the genesis of the firm. In particular we refer to the seminal work by Coase (1937), later developed in Williamson (1986), Grossman-Hart (1986), Hart-Moore (1990) and Milgrom-Roberts (1990).

Workers set up a union to save on the costs of unorganised collective defence of their interests, "co-ordination costs" in short. In the explanation of the nature of the union these costs play the same role as transaction costs for the nature of the firm. Co-ordination costs have to be borne by the workers to decide a common line of action if the union were not to be set up.

Workers face the alternative between an unorganised collective defence of their interests and the setting up of an organisation allowing to co-ordinate by delegating to a leader the authority to decide in all circumstances, which are not foreseen and so cannot be covered by an explicit agreement at the moment when the union is set up.

In other words, workers can commit only through incomplete contracts and so have to choose between bearing co-ordination costs every time they need to decide on an unforeseen contingency or facing contracts' incompleteness as a result of the delegation of authority. This delegation of authority sets up the union as a political institution, distinct from the mere sum of the workers wills.[1]

Of course, even the setting up of the union has its costs, which workers have to bear if they want to take advantage of such an organisation. From the comparison between the costs of the two alternatives the prevailing institutional setting emerges. One can imagine that in small firms with small number of workers coordination costs are low and so the setting up of a union is not needed, whereas the opposite holds in big companies with many employees.

In general, the delegation of authority will be constrained to avoid opportunistic behaviour by the delegate.

A first dimension with respect to which delegation is constrained is its width or scope, which depends on the extent of incompleteness of the potential ex-ante contract between workers, i.e. on the number of unforeseen contingencies at the moment of the union's setting up. A second constrain which is common with all the relationships of political

---

[1] With respect to the analytical representation of political institutions as incomplete contracts Persson-Roland-Tabellini (1997, p.1165) note "Real-world political constitutions are incomplete contracts: elected politicians are not offered an explicit incentive scheme associating well defined payoffs with actions in all states of the world. Political constitutions only specify who has the right to make decisions, and according to which procedures for which circumstances."

representation is the duration of the mandate. We will explicitly consider this second kind of constraint by studying a fixed-term delegation.

So far we have seen the reasons why the setting up of a union can be considered desirable for the workers. However, it seems important to further investigate the matter in order to see how alternative settings of the delegation of authority within unions can affect the outcome of the bargaining between unions and firms. In particular, it seems interesting to see the difference between choosing a union leader between workers and selecting a professional for that job. In the latter case delegation may, and in general will, imply a distortion of the delegate preferences from the members', so that selecting a professional correspond to using strategic delegation.

In the next sections we analyse a modified version of a model by Moene (1988), in order to compare two alternative settings of the union with respect to the problem of credibility of the choice of industrial actions.

In the first of these settings, labelled direct bargaining, the appointed union leader is one of the workers and so have the same incentive structure as the fellow workers. So, he has to bear all the costs of the possible industrial actions, which might be selected during the bargaining process.

The alternative setting we consider involves a strategic delegation to a professional leader, who does not need to bear the costs of industrial actions.

4.3   A model of bargaining with threats

In the previous section we have seen how the delegation to a leader may emerge as an efficient organisational setting to defend workers interests. One of the main tasks of a union leader is to bargain with firms or firms organisation on wages. In order to study how delegation may affect bargaining with firms, in this section we briefly introduce a model of wage and employment determination, which is a simple version of Moene (1988).[2] The model can be interpreted as representing bargaining at the

---

[2] The way in which we model the bargaining between unions and firms is commonly used in the literature. Classical references are MacDonald-Solow (1981) and Oswald (1985).

national level, between national unions and firms organisations, or at the local level, between the single firm and the local union. For simplicity we will refer to the two bargaining players as "firm" and "union", but most of what we say can be applied also at the national level.

We assume that the relationships between workers and firms are regulated by contract of finite duration. At the end of the period when the contract holds, firms choose the number of workers they want to hire and then bargain with the union a new contract, which establish a new wage. This is the sequence of moves which is prevailing in Europe and it is also justified by the lower degree of reversibility of the choice of the number of workers to employ with respect to the choice of the wage.

As long as the bargaining process fails to reach an outcome, union can choose to implement one of the two following industrial action to exercise pressure on the firm. It can either choose to go on strike (s) or to implement "work to rule" (sb), while the bargaining process goes on. All the workers participate in the industrial action once they are decided. The bargaining process has a finite length, equal to the normal duration of the contract, of T periods.

The firm has a per period revenue function $R(L)$, increasing and concave in the number of employees, L, i.e. $R'(L) > 0$ and $R''(L) < 0$. It sells its products in a perfectly competitive market. Its profit function is the following:

$$\Pi = R(L) - wL \tag{4.1}$$

where w is the workers' wage.

On the union side the bargaining party is an elected leader, who can be alternatively either one the workers or a professional. We assume that on both cases the union leader is only interested in maximising wage.[3]

We represent the situation just described in the following game.

---

[3] In any case, the sequential structure of the game does not leave to the union any possibility to affect the determination of the number of employees, since that choice is made by the firm before the bargaining on wage.

Game 4.1

Stage 1. The firm chooses the number of workers to employ in order to maximise its profit

$$\max_{L} \Pi = R(L) - wL \tag{4.1a}$$

$$L \geq 0^{\,4}$$

Stage 2. The wage is determined through a bargaining process, which involves a finite sequence of offers and counter-offers by the two parties, one for each bargaining periods T. At the beginning of each period a random mechanism determines who, between the union and the firm, will make the offer.[5] Once an offer has been made, it is considered by the counterpart, which can accept o reject it. If the offer is accepted, then the bargaining process stops. If it is rejected, the union decides whether to implement an industrial action in the next period and which one to choose. Then, the bargaining process goes on and the party, which makes the offer in the next period, is randomly selected.

Moene (1988) shows that the equilibrium of such a bargaining game corresponds to the solution of the following generalised Nash bargaining problem

$$\max_{w} \left[R(L) - wL - \Pi^{\circ} \right]^{\alpha} \left(w - w^{\circ} \right)^{1-\alpha} \tag{4.2}$$

where $0 < \alpha < 1$ is a measure of the relative bargaining power of the parties, Π° and w° are the disagreement payoffs of the firm and the union, i.e. how much the firm and the bargaining subject on the union side, i.e. its leader,

---

[4] The interpretation of the non-negativity constraint on the number of workers is obvious. The case when $L=0$, although it is taken account of, is not particularly interesting for the present analysis.

[5] As it is well known the sequence of moves affects the equilibrium of a bargaining game *à la* Rubinstein (Rubinstein, 1982), as the one considered. In particular, the player who moves first has an advantage on its rival. As a consequence in each period the players will compete to be the first who makes an offer. As it was first suggested by Hoel (1987), it seems reasonable to assume that the identity of the player who makes the first move is randomly determined. This becomes even more appropriate in this setting where delegation allows the union to decide as quickly as the firm.

get when bargaining is interrupted and the union implements one of the industrial actions at its disposal.

The equilibrium wage has to ensure that both parties can get at least how much they are able to get not signing any agreement. The division of the surplus in excess of the disagreement payoffs depends on the bargaining power of the parties.

Moene shows that in the subgame perfect equilibrium of Game 4.1 the wage is the following

$$w^* = (1-\alpha)\left[\frac{R(L)-\Pi^\circ}{L}\right] + \alpha\, w^\circ \tag{4.3}$$

while the number of employees is obtained by substituting (4.3) into (4.1a) and solving the first order condition.

Therefore, both the equilibrium wage and the number of employees depend on both the disagreement payoffs of the parties and so on the industrial actions selected by the union leader. In particular, the equilibrium wage decreases as the firm's disagreement payoff increases, i.e. it is lower for industrial actions, which damage less the firm:

$$\frac{dw^*}{d\Pi^\circ} = -\frac{1-\alpha}{L} < 0. \tag{4.4}$$

A rise in w° has a clear positive direct effect on w^*, and so a negative effect on the number of employed workers. However, a reduction in the number of employed workers has an uncertain effect on the equilibrium wage and so the overall effect on w^* of changes in w° is uncertain as well.

Therefore, in this setting it is always worthwhile for the union to threat to use industrial actions, which damage the firm most in terms of a reduction in profit. On the other hand it is uncertain whether the union finds it useful to minimise the workers burden of a possible industrial action.

However, it might be useful to stress that in this kind of models, under perfect information, as in this case, in equilibrium no threat is really implemented. It is just the threat, when it is credible, to affect the outcome of the bargaining game.

4.4   Direct bargaining

In order to fully characterise the equilibrium of Game 4.1 it is necessary to define the disagreement payoffs of the parties for both the case of strike and of "work to rule".[6] This in turn depends on how the workers have organised the collective defence of their interests, i.e. on the way they have chosen to organise the union. In this section we assume that the union leader is not a professional but one of the workers. In so doing our analysis coincides with some of the cases discussed by Moene (1988), whose results we summarise for convenience.

During a strike the firm does not produce anything and so it has no revenue and no cost, since no wage is paid. The workers get a strike subsidy from the union equal to z, smaller than w_r, the wage level at the beginning of the bargaining process.

Then the disagreement payoffs will be:

$$\Pi_s^o = 0 \; [7] \tag{4.5}$$

$$w_s^o = z. \tag{4.6}$$

"Work to rule", by causing a reduction in the production capacity used, implies a reduction in revenues. On the other hand, with "work to rule" the firm has still to pay the wage w_r, since the workers formally fulfil their contractual duties.

Then the disagreement payoffs with "work to rule" will be:

$$\Pi_{sb}^o = \theta R(L) - w_r L \tag{4.7}$$

---

[6] Note that "the case of" really means "the case when the credible threat is", since, as mentioned above, in equilibrium threats are not really implemented. The same holds for similar expressions.

[7] The assumption of zero-profit in case of strike disregards both the possibility that employers associations may decide to subsidise firms in that circumstance and the existence of capital depreciation costs. Taking those into account would change the bargaining power of firms without substantially modifying the main results of our analysis.

$$w_{sb}^{\,\circ} = w_r \tag{4.8}$$

where $0 < \theta < 1$ is a coefficient for the extent by which the revenues are reduced.

Through "work to rule" the union reduces the disagreement payoff of the firm without cuts in wage. Then, this industrial action is strictly better than the alternative not to use any, which is always available but can, for that reason, be disregarded.

By substituting (4.5) and (4.6) first, and (4.7) and (4.8) then into (4.1a) and (4.2) we can calculate the equilibrium conditions of the game in both cases and compare them with respect to the equilibrium wage and number of employees.

Let us call L_s and L_{sb} the number of employees in the case of strike and work to rule. The equilibrium wage in the case of strike is

$$w_s^* = (1-\alpha)\frac{R(L_s)}{L_s} + \alpha z \tag{4.9}$$

where w_s^* is an average, weighted by the parties bargaining powers, of the average productivity of workers and of the strike subsidy.

For "work to rule" the equilibrium wage is

$$w_{sb}^* = (1-\alpha)(1-\theta)\frac{R(L_{sb})}{L_{sb}} + w_r \tag{4.10}$$

i.e. the wage at the beginning of the bargaining process augmented by a sum directly proportional to the productivity of the workers with "work to rule" and their bargaining power.

The number of employed workers in case of strike and of "work to rule" can be obtained by equilibrium conditions (4.11) and (4.12):

$$R'(L) = z ; \tag{4.11}$$

$$R'(L) = \frac{w_r}{\alpha + (1-\alpha)\theta} . \tag{4.12}$$

Moene (1988) shows that, as a consequence of the concavity of $R(L)$, the number of employed workers with strike will be larger than with "work to rule", i.e. $L_s^* > L_{sb}^*$. Furthermore, given that, again for $R(L)$ concavity, $\dfrac{R(L_{sb})}{L_{sb}} > \dfrac{R(L_s)}{L_s}$, while $w_r > \alpha z$, if the reduction of the average productivity of the workers which follows from "work to rule" is sufficiently large, i.e. if θ is sufficiently small, the equilibrium wage with "work to rule" is larger than with strike, i.e. $w_{sb}^* > w_s^*$.

Indeed, as θ decreases the disagreement payoff of the firm with "work to rule" decreases and with it the minimum level of profit that the firm is prepared to accept as the outcome of the bargaining. Hence, as θ decreases the equilibrium wage increases. In particular $w_{sb}^* > w_s^*$ if the following condition holds

$$\theta < 1 + \frac{w_r - \alpha z}{(1-\alpha)\dfrac{R(L_{sb})}{L_{sb}}} - \frac{\dfrac{R(L_s)}{L_s}}{\dfrac{R(L_{sb})}{L_{sb}}}. \tag{4.13}$$

The choice of the number of employed workers depends on the equilibrium wage, which is determined at the second stage, but the firm anticipates at the first stage. In turn the equilibrium wage depends on the disagreement payoffs of the parties. However, as it can be noted by substituting (4.3) into (4.1a), while a change in the number of workers always has a positive effect on profit which depends on the disagreement payoff of the union, the same does not hold for the disagreement payoff of the firm, which enters to determine the equilibrium wage only as a per capita variable. The only exception to this is the case of "work to rule", when the disagreement payoff of the firm itself directly depends on L, as it can be seen from (4.7). The equilibrium number of employed workers will be reduced with "work to rule" by the firm's concern to keep its disagreement payoff as large as possible, while that concern is absent in case of strike, since the disagreement payoff of the firm is equal to zero and does not depend on the number of workers.

On top of this there is the effect on wage of the difference between the disagreement payoffs of the union in the two cases, which further reduces L_{sb}^* with respect to L_s^*.[8]

In this model of direct bargaining, i.e. without strategic delegation to a professional leader, "work to rule" turns out to be better than strike as a bargaining threat with respect to the objective of maximising the equilibrium wage, while strike is shown to be more effective in order to maximise the number of employed workers.

In order to be effective in determining the wage level and the number of employed workers, the threat of implementing an industrial action has to be credible, i.e. it has to be the equilibrium strategy when the bargaining process gets to a standstill.

If the union can commit to a strategy determined ex-ante, the choice between industrial actions is determined by their effect on the equilibrium of the whole bargaining game. If commitment is not an available option, the announcement that the ex-ante optimal strategy will be implemented is not credible. In that case the equilibrium industrial action will be selected as the non-co-operative equilibrium of the game which follows a standstill in the bargaining process, which is optimal ex-post and so credible.[9]

In the case under scrutiny in this section we assume that commitment is not available. The strike subsidy, z, is lower than the wage when the bargaining starts, w_r. Then, if the workers decide, the equilibrium industrial action will be "work to rule", which guarantees to workers a higher level of income. However, if workers, as it has been assumed, are only interested to wages, the threat of working to rule is not only credible because it is optimal ex-post, but it is also optimal ex-ante. Then, we can state the following proposition, equivalent to a result in Moene (1988):

---

[8] Analytically, the effect which depends on the firm's disagreement payoff can be seen by writing the profit function for the case of "work to rule", i.e. by substituting (4.7) and (4.8) into (4.1a), as follows $\Pi_{sb}=\alpha[R(L_{sb})-w_rL]+(1-\alpha)[\theta\ R(L_{sb})-w_rL]$. Given concavity of $R(L)$, it is obvious that the value of L which maximises $\alpha[R(L_{sb})-w_rL]$, (equivalent to the profit function if we disregard the effect of the firm's disagreement payoff) is larger than that maximising $(1-\alpha)[\theta\ R(L_{sb})-w_rL]$.

[9] On the problem of selection of the strategy when bargaining gets to a standstill, see Myerson, (1991), p.385.

Proposition 4.1. In the equilibrium of Game 4.1, with direct bargaining the equilibrium wage is

$$w^*_{sb} = (1-\alpha)(1-\theta)\frac{R(L_{sb})}{L_{sb}} + w_r$$

the number of employed workers satisfies

$$R'(L) = \frac{w_r}{\alpha + (1-\alpha)\theta}$$

and the union credible threat is "work to rule".

When the union leader is a worker, the threat of the implementation of the strongest industrial actions, as the strike, is not credible. Indeed those actions, although they hurt the firm most, are also very costly for the workers themselves. Softer industrial action, such as "work to rule", are selected by the workers, because they are less or not at all costly in terms of reduction in income. This very feature, making less unpleasant for workers the use of industrial actions, strengthen the workers bargaining power and allow them to get a higher wage. As a consequence of the need to pay a higher wage, the firm will hire fewer workers in this equilibrium than in the case when harsher industrial actions are credible threats. This also allows the firm to increase its disagreement payoff and to further improve its position during the bargaining process.

4.5   Strategically delegated bargaining

In this section we consider the case when the bargaining party on the union side is a professional leader. He is given the objective to maximise wage, but he does not directly bear the costs of industrial actions planned for the case when the bargaining process gets to a standstill.

For simplicity we assume that the union leader cannot be replaced before the official end of his mandate, or alternatively that the replacement is infinitely costly, and that delegation cannot be renewed to the same person.[10]

Our analysis considers the effects of a fixed term strategic delegation to a professional leader on wage determination. The possibility of strategic manipulation of the delegate's preferences through incentive contracts is ruled out.[11] Hence, we will concentrate on the possibility to strategically delegate by appropriately selecting the person whom to delegate to.

It is now crucial to establish which is the disagreement payoff of the professional leader, while the disagreement payoffs of the firm depends as before on which of the union's threats turns out to be credible. Professional union leaders does not need to bear the costs of industrial actions, so that for example they do not get directly damaged by choosing to go on strike, while members in that case have their salaries reduced.

Therefore, the disagreement payoff of a professional union leader is invariant with respect to the kind of industrial action chosen and it is equal to an arbitrary value that we call ω:

$$w_s^\circ = w_{sb}^\circ = \omega . \tag{4.14}$$

As a consequence strike, "work to rule" and any other industrial action are all equally credible threats, because they all belong to the set of optimal strategies for the union leader. Among all those strategies the leader will then choose the most effective. So, at difference with the case of direct bargaining, the delegation to a professional leader makes the threat of strike optimal ex-ante to become also optimal ex-post.

The disagreement payoff of the union is the lower bound for the offer acceptable by the bargaining agent. In the case of a professional leader, its invariance with respect to the industrial actions used does not allow per se to unambiguously determine its level.

---

[10] These simplifying assumptions do not make the analysis loose its generality, because the results are qualitatively the same when the assumptions are removed.

[11] However, remember that, as shown by Osborne-Rubinstein (1990), in this setting in order to affect wage determination strategic delegation through incentive contracts has to distort the degree of risk aversion of the leader away from the workers'. Indeed, the equilibrium wage in (4.2) does not change for any affine transformation of the objective function of any of the parties, while it increases (decreases) if the degree of risk aversion of the person in charge of the bargaining process.

However, an obvious minimal restriction to be imposed on the professional leader's disagreement payoff is that it is not lower than the wage at the beginning of the bargaining process. That corresponds to requiring that the leader will not accept any offer below that wage level. An artificial raise of the lower bound of the set of the counterpart's offers acceptable to the union would allow the union to strategically strengthen its bargaining position, as shown by Muthoo (1992). However this possibility is not considered in this chapter.

Hence, we limit ourselves to consider the alternative which is less favourable for the union, i.e. that corresponding to a lower equilibrium wage and to a disagreement payoff of the leader always identical to the wage at the beginning of the bargaining process, i.e.

$$w_s^{\circ} = w_{sb}^{\circ} = \omega = w_r \tag{4.15}$$

It is important to note however, that for our main results to hold, the disagreement payoffs do not need to be represented by (4.15): it is enough that they are invariant with respect to the industrial action chosen.

Proceeding in our analysis, we note that in the present case of delegated bargaining, the disagreement payoffs of the firm stay the same as for direct bargaining ((4.5) and (4.7)). By substituting w_r to w° in (4.2) and solving the game in the case of delegated bargaining we get the following equilibrium wage for strike and "work to rule":

$$w_s^* = (1-\alpha)\frac{R(L_s)}{L_s} + \alpha w_r \tag{4.16}$$

$$w_{sb}^* = (1-\alpha)(1-\theta)\frac{R(L_{sb})}{L_{sb}} + w_r . \tag{4.17}$$

With respect to the case of direct bargaining the equilibrium wage corresponding to "work to rule" stays the same, the increase in the disagreement payoff for the strike has a positive effect on the corresponding equilibrium wage, both directly and indirectly through a reduction of the number of employed workers. The corresponding levels of employment are determined for both cases by solving the following equilibrium condition:

$$R'(L) = w_r ; \tag{4.18}$$

$$R'(L) = \frac{w_r}{\alpha + (1-\alpha)\theta}.$$ (4.19)

Given that $\theta < 1$ and $0 < \alpha < 1$, then $\alpha + (1-\alpha)\theta < 1$. For concavity of the revenue function the number of employed with strike will then be larger than for "work to rule", even though by a smaller difference than with direct bargaining, since $\dfrac{w_r}{\alpha + (1-\alpha)\theta} > w_r > z$.

In order to compare the two equilibrium wages we subtract (4.17) from (4.16) and, after a few simplifications, we get:

$$w_s^* - w_{sb}^* = (1-\alpha)\left[-w_r + \frac{R(L_s)}{L_s} - \frac{R(L_{sb})}{L_{sb}}(1-\theta) \right].$$ (4.20)

Hence, the equilibrium wage with the strike will be larger than with "work to rule" if the following holds

$$\theta > 1 + \frac{w_r - \dfrac{R(L_s)}{L_s}}{\dfrac{R(L_{sb})}{L_{sb}}}.$$ (4.21)

The right hand side is always smaller than 1, because $w_r < \dfrac{R(L_s)}{L_s}$.

Therefore, there are cases where (4.21) is satisfied and $w_s^* > w_{sb}^*$. In particular, this is possible when the negative effect of "work to rule" on revenues is sufficiently small, i.e. when θ is sufficiently large. In that case the threat of strike is both in the set of optimal ex-post strategies and ex-ante optimum, since it allows to maximise the equilibrium wage, which is assumed to be the only objective of the workers.

This happens because the delegation to a professional implies that the disagreement payoff of a strike is not lower than with "work to rule" and so the credibility of that threat does not reduce the minimum wage offer acceptable by the union. Instead, with direct bargaining (as in Moene

(1988)) the strike turned out to be better than "work to rule" with respect to employment, but not in term of wage.

Then we can state the following proposition:

Proposition 4.2. In the equilibrium of game 4.1, in the case of delegated bargaining to a professional leader, if

$$\theta > 1 + \frac{w_r - \dfrac{R(L_s)}{L_s}}{\dfrac{R(L_{sb})}{L_{sb}}}$$

the equilibrium wage is

$$w_s^* = (1-\alpha)\frac{R(L_s)}{L_s} + \alpha w_r$$

the number of employed workers satisfies the following condition

$$R'(L) = w_r$$

and the credible threat of the union, if the bargaining process gets to a standstill is the strike.

Finally, we compare the equilibrium of delegated bargaining (Proposition 4.2) with that of direct bargaining of the previous section (Proposition 4.1). From the comparison between (4.12) and (4.18), it emerges that the number of employed is larger with delegated bargaining, since

$$\frac{w_r}{\alpha + (1-\alpha)\theta} > w_r . \tag{4.22}$$

From (4.10), (4.16) and (4.17), we can verify that the equilibrium wage with delegated bargaining is larger than with direct bargaining if (4.21) holds, since the wage for "work to rule" is the same in the two organisational settings of the union. We can then state the following proposition:

Proposition 4.3. In Game 4.1, if

$$\theta > 1 + \frac{w_r - \dfrac{R(L_s)}{L_s}}{\dfrac{R(L_{sb})}{L_{sb}}}$$

the equilibrium in the case of delegated bargaining is characterised by larger wage and number of employed workers than with direct bargaining.

By comparing (4.21) with (4.13) we note that the lower bound on θ in (4.21) is smaller than the upper bound in (4.13), i.e. that

$$1 + \frac{w_r - \dfrac{R(L_{sd})}{L_{sd}}}{\dfrac{R(L_{sb})}{L_{sb}}} < 1 + \frac{w_r - \alpha z}{(1-\alpha)\dfrac{R(L_{sb})}{L_{sb}}} - \frac{\dfrac{R(L_s)}{L_s}}{\dfrac{R(L_{sb})}{L_{sb}}} \qquad (4.23)$$

where, with a light abuse of notation, we used sd to refer to the case of strike with delegated bargaining to distinguish it from the case of strike with direct bargaining which is simply referred to as s. (4.23) is satisfied, because $\dfrac{w_r}{\dfrac{R(L_{sb})}{L_{sb}}} < \dfrac{w_r - \alpha z}{(1-\alpha)\dfrac{R(L_{sb})}{L_{sb}}}$ and $\dfrac{R(L_{sd})}{L_{sd}} > \dfrac{R(L_s)}{L_s}$, given that

$w_r > z$ and the number of employed in case of strike with delegated bargaining is smaller than the number of employed in case of strike with direct bargaining. Hence, when the capability to reduce the firm's revenues through "work to rule" is large, i.e. when θ is very small, the equilibrium wage with "work to rule" will be larger than with strike for all the organisational settings of the union, which turns out to be indifferent for the workers. For intermediate values of θ, between

$$1 + \frac{w_r - \dfrac{R(L_{sd})}{L_{sd}}}{\dfrac{R(L_{sb})}{L_{sb}}} \quad \text{and} \quad 1 + \frac{w_r - \alpha z}{(1-\alpha)\dfrac{R(L_{sb})}{L_{sb}}} - \frac{\dfrac{R(L_s)}{L_s}}{\dfrac{R(L_{sb})}{L_{sb}}}, \text{ strike guarantees}$$

a higher wage with delegated bargaining, while with direct bargaining the wage with "work to rule" is higher. As shown in Proposition 4.3, within this interval workers prefer delegated bargaining.

Finally, if "work to rule is very ineffective in damaging the firm, i.e. if

$$\theta > 1 + \frac{w_r - \alpha z}{(1-\alpha)\dfrac{R(L_{sb})}{L_{sb}}} - \frac{\dfrac{R(L_s)}{L_s}}{\dfrac{R(L_{sb})}{L_{sb}}}, \text{ the strike always provides a higher}$$

wage so that delegated bargaining is better.

From the analysis of this section it emerges that the delegation of bargaining decisions to a professional union leader is better for workers only concerned with wage. If the workers' ability to reduce the firm revenues by working to rule is not too large, the professional leader can use the threat of strike to get a higher wage than that obtainable with direct bargaining, since the workers are unable to credibly threat a strike. Given that the number of employed workers in case of strike is always larger than with "work to rule", delegation to a professional leader may turn out to be better for the objective of maximising the total surplus of the production activity. Therefore, that organisational setting not only assures a private benefit to the workers, but also in some cases maximises social welfare.

4.6   Conclusions

In this chapter we have analysed strategic delegation in a trade union bargaining with a firm on wage setting. We have studied how the union can be represented as a political institution where the authority is delegated to a leader. We have shown that workers can find it profitable to strategically delegate authority to a professional leader, who does not need to bear the costs of industrial actions. This allows to credibly commit to implement threats, which are at the same time effective but costly for the workers.

In particular, we considered the alternative between two industrial actions: strike and "work to rule". If "work to rule" is much less effective and less costly than a strike, a union lead by a professional will use the strike as a credible threat, while a union lead by a worker will use "work to rule". The equilibrium wage and the number of employed workers will be larger under a professional leadership, so that this organisational setting may turn out to be both privately optimal for workers and social welfare maximising.

The present analysis has then shown that strategic delegation is not only a profitable organisational arrangement for firms or a useful way to design institution in charge of monetary policy, as it was already well known from previous literature. It also turns out to be valuable in increasing the organisational effectiveness of the trade union in defending workers' interests.

Chapter 5 - Competition for delegates and the evolution of market structure

5.1 New managers, technological innovation and industry evolution[°]

In previous chapters, we considered different settings where strategic delegation is used by principals to change the equilibrium outcomes of the delegated games. However, the payoff structure of such games is not changed by the act of delegation itself. In this chapter, I study the case where the act of delegation changes the delegated game's payoffs, so that a sequence of delegation decisions have a dynamic effect, shaping the evolution of the strategic interaction that the principal is involved in. Principals compete between each other to acquire new delegates as they become available, and this competition modifies their relative strategic strength over time.

As an example of such a phenomenon, we study the effect of competition for acquiring new managers, as they become available in the labour market, on the evolution of the product market structure in duopoly when manager's contributions to the firms may be in different degrees of complementarity/substitutibility. We model competition for managers as a finite sequence of races, where the effect of a new manager on a firm may change with the number of managers previously working with that firm.

[°] I am grateful to Michael Luck for very useful help with computer simulations. A previous version was presented at the 27th Annual Conference of the European Association for Research in Industrial Economics, Université de Lausanne, September 7-10 2000.

Managers may show different degrees of complementarity/substitutability between each other. There may be a multiplicative effect, so that a manager produces a larger efficiency gain if hired by a firm with more managers. Alternatively, the benefits from a new manager for a certain firm may decrease as the number of managers it has increases. Finally, new managers might affect different firms in exactly the same way, by reducing the costs of firms with a different number of managers by the same amount. Therefore, different degrees of complementarity and substitutability among managers influence the patterns of returns to managers, and so determine the outcome of races to acquire them and the evolution of market structure.

The present analysis has the same basic structure of models studying the relationship between technological innovation and the evolution of product market competition which have been surveyed by Beath, Katsoulacos and Ulph (1995). The hiring of new managers in our setting plays the same role as innovation in that literature, which is the main reference of our work and so we briefly recap its main results.

According to Beath, Katsoulacos and Ulph (1995) the relationship between product market competition and technological innovation is twofold: on one hand the outcome of technological competition determines the production possibility set of the firms and so influences their product market behaviour; on the other, the features of product market competition affect the firms' incentives for innovation.

With respect to the latter, two main forces have been identified in the literature as providing firms with reasons to innovate: the "profit incentive" and the "competitive threat". The profit incentive is the increase in a firm's profit directly brought about by a successful innovation. This corresponds to "the incentive that would face a firm that was taking the decision in isolation" (Beath, Katsoulacos and Ulph, 1995, p.133). The profit incentive is the key incentive considered in Arrow (1962) and in non-tournament models of innovation, like Dasgupta and Stiglitz (1980) and Beath and Ulph (1990), where many different firms are able to obtain the same innovation.

On the other hand, the competitive threat is the incentive brought about by strategic competition among firms. It corresponds to a firm's potential loss, occurring if its rivals win the competition to innovate. This effect is at the core of the analysis of tournament models for both process and product innovation. In these models firms compete among them to obtain the exclusive use of a (normally patented) innovation. This excludability makes this class of models particularly suitable to study the effect of technological competition on market structure. In particular, they try to answer the question on whether under the competition for innovation the product market leader will retain/increase her dominance or rivals will catch-up/overtake her.

An important distinction among tournament models is related to the size (or speed) of innovation. An innovation can be drastic, and so allow the innovator to become a monopolist in the product market; it can allow leap-frogging, so that the firm with the less efficient technology before the competition for a new patent becomes the most efficient if it wins. Finally, innovations may just allow the less efficient to catch up on the market leader.

A further distinction among tournament models is that between models which analyse the competition for a single innovation and models contemplating sequences of innovations; furthermore, models of both kinds are set in either a certainty framework, like Vickers (1986), Delbono (1989), and Beath, Katsoulacos and Ulph (1987), or under uncertainty, like Reinganum (1985), Harris and Vickers (1987), Budd, Vickers and Harris (1993).

Beath, Katsoulacos and Ulph (1995) in a certainty setting and Reinganum (1985) in a model with uncertainty show that drastic process innovation will result in the less efficient firm taking the market leadership, i.e. in a creative destruction or action/reaction outcome. Leap-frogging tends in general to favour action/reaction, since the leader can always be overtaken by her rivals. This is shown to be the case in a model of a sequence of patent races under certainty by Vickers (1986) for Cournot product market competition and linear demand, and by Beath, Katsoulacos and Ulph (1995) when the outcome of the innovative activity is uncertain. Finally, catch-up models of certainty, like Delbono (1989), and of uncertainty, like Harris and Vickers (1987), show that small innovations foster persistent/increasing dominance.

Delbono (1989) provides the most direct predecessor to the present study by modelling the evolution of duopoly with catch-up innovations and patent races which are history dependent, since the level of technological efficiency of a firm depends on the number of patents it holds and not only on the last one it got, as, for instance, in Vickers (1986). Delbono only considers the case of constant returns to patents and make the equilibrium price of patents independent from the evolution of firms' incentives to win the races by introducing into the analysis a participation cost.

The analysis of this chapter is phrased and interpreted as describing a particular sort of process innovation. Beath, Katsoulacos and Ulph (1987) provides an analysis of industry evolution under the alternative setting of product innovation. They show that action/reaction prevails if the speed of innovation is high, while persistent dominance is the outcome for slow technological change.

In this chapter the improvement in firms' profitability obtained through the hiring of a new manager corresponds to the speed (or alternatively the size) of innovation. It varies with the history of the firms, so that the returns on new managers may be non-constant and their effects may be different among firms. This is shown to affect the equilibrium pattern of evolution of the market and to decrease the number of cases where dominance increases.

In section 2 we present the main features of the model with particular reference to the mechanism of allocation of managers between firms. Section 3 introduces sufficient conditions for Catching-Up to be the prevailing pattern of the evolution of the market, while in section 4 analogous conditions are studied for Increasing Dominance. In section 5 the case of the evolution of a linear Cournot duopoly with non-constant returns to managers and different degrees of product differentiation is studied. Section 6 explores the evolution of incentives with decreasing returns to managers both through an analytical discussion and some simulations. Section 7 illustrates the implications of the equilibrium evolution on social welfare. Section 8 concludes.

5.2   A model of dynamic competition for managers

We model competition for managers as a finite sequence of $1,...,t,...,T$ races between firm A and firm B operating in a duopolistic product market. Both firms have constant marginal costs $c_i(x)$, $i = A$, B, where x is the number of managers a firm has. Each firm's marginal costs are lower the greater the number of managers it has, which we label m for firm A and n for firm B, i.e. $x=m,n$. Hence we have:

$$c_A = c(m) \qquad c_A(m+1) < c_A(m) \tag{5.1}$$

$$c_B = c(n) \qquad c_B(n+1) < c_B(n) \tag{5.1a}$$

Apart from the number of managers they have, the two firms are perfectly identical, so that $c_A(x) = c_B(x) = c(x)$ for the same x. Production costs depend on the number of managers a firm has, and not only on the last one it got, but the timing and the sequence of the acquisition of the managers do not matter.

At the beginning of each period t a new manager becomes available and firms compete for that manager in a second price auction, so that the firm that makes the highest bid wins the manager and pays the value attached to the manager by its rival. In each period, after the manager is allocated the firms play the market game by choosing the quantities to produce, q_A and q_B or the prices, p_A and p_B.

Let $\pi(m,n)$ and $\pi(n,m)$ be the one-period profit for firm A and firm B, when they have respectively m and n managers, and $\sigma(m,n)$ the corresponding joint profits. $\pi(\cdot,\cdot)$ is strictly increasing in its first argument and decreasing in its second. For each firm, the incentive to win the manager race in a certain period depends not only on the profit obtainable in that period, but also on the foreseeable outcome of the following periods. Therefore, the incentive to win is represented in terms of continuation payoffs, i.e. the sum of all future profits net of the costs of managers.

Denote by m_t and n_t the number of managers A and B have at the end of period t, whichever is the winner of the race. Let $\omega(m_{t-1} + 1, n_{t-1})$ be the continuation payoff of firm A from winning race t; $\omega(m_{t-1} + 1, n_{t-1})$ is the sum of A's profit in period t and the profits it is going to make in the continuation of the game net of the payments for the managers it is going to win in periods after t (but excluding the payment for the manager won in period t).

The winner of any race is the firm that gets the largest increment in its continuation payoff when winning, i.e. has the highest valuation in that race. Therefore, firm A wins race t if the following holds:

$$\omega(m_{t-1} + 1, n_{t-1}) - \omega(m_{t-1}, n_{t-1} + 1) > \omega(n_{t-1} + 1, m_{t-1}) - \omega(n_{t-1}, m_{t-1} + 1)$$
(5.2)

Firm B wins if the reverse holds.

It is easy to see that condition (5.2) can be re-written in terms of joint continuation payoff, denoted by $\tau(\cdot,\cdot)$:

$$\tau(m_{t-1} + 1, n_{t-1}) > \tau(n_{t-1} + 1, m_{t-1})$$
(5.3)

where $\tau(m,n)=\omega(m,n)+\omega(n,m)$. If firm A wins the race in period t, its net benefit is

$$\omega(m_{t-1}+1,n_{t-1})-[\omega(n_{t-1}+1,m_{t-1})-\omega(n_{t-1},m_{t-1}+1)]$$

(5.4)

This is the difference between firm A's continuation payoff if it wins and the payment it has to make, i.e. its rival's evaluation of the same manager.

On the other hand, the net benefit for firm B from losing is simply its continuation payoff:

$$\omega(n_{t-1},m_{t-1}+1).$$

(5.4a)

The net benefit in (5.4) is added to $\pi(m_{t-1},\ n_{t-1})$ to obtain firm A's continuation payoff for ending up with m_{t-1} managers in the previous period, while (5.4a) is added to $\pi(n_{t-1},\ m_{t-1})$ to get B's continuation payoff. In general, the continuation payoff can be written as follows:

$$\omega(m,n)=\pi(n,m)+max\{\omega(m+1,n)-[\omega(n+1,m)-\omega(n,m+1)],\omega(m,n+1)\}$$

(5.5)

If we keep our provisional assumption that firm A wins in period t, and we move back to period $t-1$, we can then write

$$\tau(m_{t-2}+1,n_{t-2})=\sigma(m_{t-2}+1,n_{t-2})+\tau(m_{t-1}+1,n_{t-1})$$
$$-[\omega(n_{t-1}+1,m_{t-1})-\omega(n_{t-1},m_{t-1}+1)]$$

(5.6)

whose general form is, from *(5.5)*,

$$\tau(m,n)=\sigma(m,n)+max\left\{\begin{array}{l}\tau(m+1,n)-[\omega(n+1,m)-\omega(n,m+1)],\\ \tau(m,n+1)-[\omega(m+1,n)-\omega(m,n+1)]\end{array}\right\}$$

(5.6a)

In general the left-hand side and the right-hand side of (5.3) are different, so that a winner for the race can be identified. A notable exception is when both firms have the same number of managers, i.e. $m_{t-1}=n_{t-1}$, given that we assumed the firms are identical. In that case $\tau(m_{t-1}+1,n_{t-1})=\tau(n_{t-1}+1,m_{t-1})$ and there is no obvious criterion to decide which firm wins the race. Hence we may assume a purely random allocation as a tiebreak rule.

However, it is important to notice that in a race starting with the firms holding an equal number of managers there is no gain for the winner. This is a consequence of the valuations of the two firms being the same and can be seen by imposing the condition $m_{t-1}=n_{t-1}$ to (5.4) and (5.4a). If $m_{t-1}=n_{t-1}$ then $\omega(m_{t-1}+1,n_{t-1})=\omega(n_{t-1}+1,m_{t-1})$, so that (5.4) reduces to (5.4a). Therefore, when we reach the stage in which both firms have the same number of managers, it is as if the entire game had ended. There is no advantage for either firm from being the winner, since all the present and future rents from winning go to the seller.

We notice that our problem might be formulated in a finite horizon dynamic programming format, where the control variable is the allocation of the new managers to either firm. In order to identify the equilibrium allocation of all the T managers, the model has to be solved backwards, starting from the last race, when the continuation payoff for each firm is just its profit for period T, and moving towards the first one to identify the sub-game perfect equilibrium of the game. Characterising the solution for the general case of this model, while not impossible in principle, is not rewarding, even when we choose particular functional forms for the cost and the demand functions. Results can be obtained through numerical simulations. Furthermore, the corresponding infinite horizon problem has no stationary structure, so that a recursive solution cannot be found.

Following the approach used by Vickers (1986) and Delbono (1989), we will concentrate on determining sufficient conditions for Catching-Up (CU), when the firm which has fewer managers at the beginning of the race wins, and Increasing Dominance (ID), when the other firm wins. Then we study whether and when either of these conditions is satisfied under different assumptions on the complementarity-substitutability between, and so on the returns to, managers.

Hereafter, we will call "leader" the firm with more managers at the beginning of the race and "follower" the other.

5.3   Catching-Up

In this section we derive sufficient conditions for CU to prevail in all periods of the game, following the procedure used in Vickers (1986) and Delbono (1989). Let us start from the last period T. In period T the joint continuation value corresponds to joint profits, since there is no continuation afterwards. Therefore, the follower wins the last race if the following conditions hold:

$$\sigma\left(m_{T-1}+1,n_{T-1}\right)>\sigma\left(m_{T-1},n_{T-1}+1\right) \quad \text{for } m_{T-1}<n_{T-1}$$

$$(5.7)$$

$$\sigma\left(m_{T-1}+1,n_{T-1}\right)<\sigma\left(m_{T-1},n_{T-1}+1\right) \quad \text{for } m_{T-1}>n_{T-1}$$

Notice that when $m_{T-1} = n_{T-1}$, we have already assumed that random allocation takes place.

Conditions (5.7) can be written also in terms of profits as

$$\pi\left(m_{T-1}+1,n_{T-1}\right)-\pi\left(m_{T-1},n_{T-1}+1\right)>\pi\left(n_{T-1}+1,m_{T-1}\right)-\pi\left(n_{T-1},m_{T-1}+1\right)$$

for $m_{T-1}<n_{T-1}$

$$(5.8)$$

$$\pi\left(m_{T-1}+1,n_{T-1}\right)-\pi\left(m_{T-1},n_{T-1}+1\right)<\pi\left(n_{T-1}+1,m_{T-1}\right)-\pi\left(n_{T-1},m_{T-1}+1\right)$$

for $m_{T-1}>n_{T-1}$.

Now we move back to a generic period $t<T$ and provisionally assume that in all the periods between $t+1$ and T CU prevails also off the equilibrium path. In period t CU prevails if the following conditions hold:

$$\tau\left(m_{t-1}+1,n_{t-1}\right)>\tau\left(m_{t-1},n_{t-1}+1\right) \quad \text{for } m_{t-1}<n_{t-1}$$

$$(5.9)$$

$$\tau\left(m_{t-1}+1,n_{t-1}\right)<\tau\left(m_{t-1},n_{t-1}+1\right) \quad \text{for } m_{t-1}>n_{t-1}$$

We examine the case $m_{t-1} < n_{t-1}$ in detail; the same considerations apply to the other. By using equation (5.6), condition (5.9) for $m_{t-1} < n_{t-1}$. can be written as follows

$$\sigma\left(m_{t-1}+1,n_{t-1}\right)+\tau\left(m_{t-1}+2,n_{t-1}\right)-\left[\omega\left(n_{t-1}+1,m_{t-1}+1\right)-\omega\left(n_{t-1},m_{t-1}+2\right)\right]>$$
$$\sigma\left(m_{t-1},n_{t-1}+1\right)+\tau\left(m_{t-1}+1,n_{t-1}+1\right)-\left[\omega\left(n_{t-1}+2,m_{t-1}\right)-\omega\left(n_{t-1}+1,m_{t-1}+1\right)\right]$$

$$(5.10)$$

Let us first consider the case in which at t the allocation of managers is so asymmetric that a symmetric allocation cannot be reached by period T. From the provisional assumption of CU prevailing in the following periods we made, we know that $\tau\left(m_{t-1}+2,n_{t-1}\right)>\tau\left(m_{t-1}+1,n_{t-1}+1\right)$. Therefore, for CU to prevail in period t it is sufficient that

$$\sigma\left(m_{t-1}+1,n_{t-1}\right)>\sigma\left(m_{t-1},n_{t-1}+1\right) \tag{5.11}$$

and

$$\omega\left(n_{t-1}+2,m_{t-1}\right)-\omega\left(n_{t-1}+1,m_{t-1}+1\right)>\omega\left(n_{t-1}+1,m_{t-1}+1\right)-\omega\left(n_{t-1},m_{t-1}+2\right) \tag{5.12}$$

Notice that (5.11) is the equivalent for period t of the top condition in (5.7) for period T, so that it can be re-written as:

$$\pi\left(m_{t-1}+1,n_{t-1}\right)-\pi\left(m_{t-1},n_{t-1}+1\right)>\pi\left(n_{t-1}+1,m_{t-1}\right)-\pi\left(n_{t-1},m_{t-1}+1\right) \tag{5.13}$$

The left hand side of (5.12) is the price firm A has to pay in order to win the race in period $t+1$ if it loses in period t, while the right hand side is the price it has to pay in period $t+1$ if it wins in period t. We consider those prices as part of the continuation values to be compared in period t, since we have provisionally assumed that from period $t+1$ on CU will prevail and firm A will win all the remaining races.

By virtue of that provisional assumption (5.12) can be re-written as follows

$$\sum_{s=0}^{T-t-1}\left[\pi\left(n_{t-1}+2,m_{t-1}+s\right)-\pi\left(n_{t-1}+1,m_{t-1}+1+s\right)\right]> \\ \sum_{s=1}^{T-t}\left[\pi\left(n_{t-1}+1,m_{t-1}+s\right)-\pi\left(n_{t-1},m_{t-1}+1+s\right)\right] \tag{5.14}$$

Therefore, CU will certainly prevail if

i) the difference in stage profit between winning and loosing is larger for the follower than for the leader in every stage;

ii) the price the follower has to pay for a manager increases with the number of managers the leader has, so that the leader cannot relax future competition by letting the rival win the present race.

We can say that the first condition refers to incentives gross of the price to pay for managers' ("gross incentives" hereafter), while the second refers to the evolution of such a price ("manager's price" in short).

We will now show that the conditions for CU we have just stated are sufficient also for the case when the initial allocation of managers allows a symmetric allocation to be reached before or at T, after k periods from t-1. Let us first consider the game at a stage when one firm (A for convenience) has just one manager less than the other, so that $m_{t-1}+1=n_{t-1}$ and $k=1$. As above (equation (5.10)), the winner of the race is established by comparing the joint continuation values for period t.

The first element of comparison is the stage joint profit, for which condition (5.13) applies. The second element of comparison is the equilibrium joint continuation payoff for period $t+1$.

As we have seen above, the outcome of the races when the allocation of managers among firms is symmetric cannot be clearly determined. Therefore, in this case the equilibrium joint continuation payoff for period $t+1$ when A wins in period t, can be either $\tau\left(m_{t-1}+2,n_{t-1}\right)$ or $\tau\left(m_{t-1}+1,n_{t-1}+1\right)$. However, from $m_{t-1}+1=n_{t-1}$ and the symmetry of $\tau(.,.)$ it follows that $\tau\left(m_{t-1}+2,n_{t-1}\right)=\tau\left(m_{t-1}+1,n_{t-1}+1\right)$, so that whichever of the two is the joint continuation payoff for period $t+1$, it does not affect the decisions at t. By assuming CU in the continuation of the game, we also know that the equilibrium joint continuation payoff for period $t+1$ when B wins in period t is $\tau\left(m_{t-1}+1,n_{t-1}+1\right)$. Therefore, in the comparison that determines the winner at t, the equilibrium continuation payoff for period $t+1$ cancel out.

The third element of comparison is the equilibrium price of period $t+1$ manager.

When A wins in period t and we have a symmetric allocation of managers, the incentive for both firms to win at $t+1$ will just involve the levels of profit at stage $t+1$, $t+2$ and $t+3$ when full symmetry is restored.

Therefore, if A wins in period t, the equilibrium price of manager $t+1$ is going to be

$$
\pi\left(m_{t-1}+2,n_{t-1}\right)-\pi\left(m_{t-1}+1,n_{t-1}+1\right)+\pi\left(m_{t-1}+3,n_{t-1}\right)-\pi\left(m_{t-1}+2,n_{t-1}+1\right)+
$$
$$
\pi\left(m_{t-1}+3,n_{t-1}+1\right)-\pi\left(m_{t-1}+2,n_{t-1}+2\right)=\pi\left(n_{t-1}+1,m_{t-1}+1\right)-\pi\left(n_{t-1},m_{t-1}+2\right)+
$$
$$
\pi\left(n_{t-1}+2,m_{t-1}+1\right)-\pi\left(n_{t-1}+1,m_{t-1}+2\right)+\pi\left(n_{t-1}+2,m_{t-1}+2\right)-\pi\left(n_{t-1}+1,m_{t-1}+3\right)
$$

$$(5.15)$$

When firm B wins in period t, a symmetric allocation of managers is going to be reached in period $t+3$. Hence, the price of manager $t+1$ is

$$\pi\left(n_{t-1}+2,m_{t-1}\right)-\pi\left(n_{t-1}+1,m_{t-1}+1\right)+\pi\left(n_{t-1}+2,m_{t-1}+1\right)$$
$$-\pi\left(n_{t-1}+1,m_{t-1}+2\right)+\pi\left(n_{t-1}+2,m_{t-1}+2\right)-\pi\left(n_{t-1}+1,m_{t-1}+3\right)$$
(5.15a)

For the condition on the price of managers to hold (5.15a) has to be greater than (5.15), which simplifies to

$$\pi\left(n_{t-1}+2,m_{t-1}\right)-\pi\left(n_{t-1}+1,m_{t-1}+1\right)>\pi\left(n_{t-1}+1,m_{t-1}+1\right)-\pi\left(n_{t-1}+1,m_{t-1}+2\right)$$
(5.15b)

The fact that a symmetric allocation of managers is reached in period t, then amounts to a reduction in the length of the sum on both sides of (5.14). In fact, the continuation payoffs for the two firms are all equal for the part corresponding to periods after full convergence is reached.

The argument generalises to the case when the difference in the initial allocation of managers between the two firms is greater than one and full converge is reached after k periods. Equation (5.14) can be generalised to take into account the possibility that the two firms reach a symmetric allocation, so that it becomes:

$$\sum_{s=0}^{T-t-1}\left[\pi\left(n_{t-1}+2,m_{t-1}+s\right)-\pi\left(n_{t-1}+1,m_{t-1}+1+s\right)\right]>$$
$$\sum_{s=1}^{T-t}\left[\pi\left(n_{t-1}+1,m_{t-1}+s\right)-\pi\left(n_{t-1},m_{t-1}+1+s\right)\right]$$

$$\text{for } m_{t-1}+T-t+1\leq n_{t-1} \qquad\qquad (5.14a)$$

when complete convergence is never reached and

$$\sum_{s=0}^{k}\left[\pi\left(n_{t-1}+2,m_{t-1}+s\right)-\pi\left(n_{t-1}+1,m_{t-1}+1+s\right)\right]>$$
$$\sum_{s=1}^{k+1}\left[\pi\left(n_{t-1}+1,m_{t-1}+s\right)-\pi\left(n_{t-1},m_{t-1}+1+s\right)\right]$$

$$\text{for } m_{t-1}+T-t+1>n_{t-1} \quad\text{and}\quad k=n_{t-1}-m_{t-1} \qquad (5.14b)$$

when complete convergence is reached after k periods.

By looking at (5.8), (5.13), (5.14a) and (5.14b) we notice that all the conditions for CU depend on the value of the difference in profit between losing and winning a race. Remembering that neither firm is able to increase its number of managers except at the expense of the other, we notice that profit functions can be written in terms only of t and either m or n, since $m=t-n$. Therefore, we are able to identify sufficient conditions for CU to prevail by studying only the shape of the following function:

$$I(x,t) = \pi(x+1, t-x-1) - \pi(x, t-x) \quad x = m, n \qquad (5.16)$$

where x is the general notation for the number of managers a firm has, either m or n, while t is the total number of managers available after race t. Function $I(x, t)$ is the difference in profit between winning and losing race t for a firm having x managers at the beginning of that race. The following lemmas provide a set of conditions jointly sufficient for $I(x, t)$ to satisfy (5.8), (5.13), (5.14a) and (5.14b) and so for CU to prevail.

Lemma 5.1. Conditions (5.14a) and (5.14b) are satisfied if

$I(x, t)$ is increasing in x for $x > (t-1)/2$.   (CU1)

Proof. Note that all elements of the sums in (5.14a) and (5.14b) are particular values of the function $I(x,t)$ and that each element on the left-hand sides has x one unit larger than the corresponding element on the right-hand sides. Also note that $m_{t-1} + T - t + 1 \le n_{t-1}$ and $m_{t-1} + k = n_{t-1}$ both imply $n > (t-1)/2$. The proof immediately follows. (QED)

(CU1) rules out the possibility that the follower finds it profitable to lose a race in order to relax future competition by reducing the leader's future incentives to win.

Lemma 5.2. Conditions (5.8) and (5.13) are satisfied if

$I(x, t) > I(t-1-x, t)$ for $x < (t-1)/2$.   (CU2)

Proof. It follows directly from inspection of equations (5.8) and (5.13). (QED)

(CU2) makes sure that the follower has greater gross incentives to win the race. As we can see from (5.7) and (5.11), (CU2) is equivalent to condition H2 in Delbono (1989), which we refer to as (CU2'):

$\sigma(m+1, n) > \sigma(m, n+1)$ for $m < n$ (CU2') although in this more general framework it turns out not to be sufficient for CU. Yet, (CU2), or (CU2'),[1] is necessary, since if it is violated, CU cannot prevail at the last stage T (see (5.7)).

(CU1) and (CU2) are jointly sufficient for CU to prevail. A sketch of the two conditions is provided in Figure 5.1 below.[2]

Figure 5.1: Conditions (CU1) and (CU2)

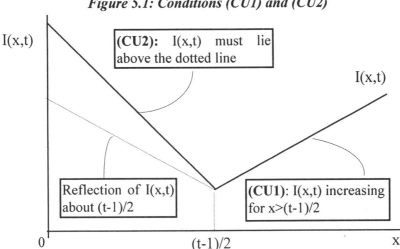

We can now summarise conditions (CU1) and (CU2) in the following proposition.

Proposition 5.3. If

i. $I(x, t)$ is increasing in x for $x > (t-1)/2$,

ii. $I(x, t) > I(t-1-x, t)$ for $x < (t-1)/2$

then manager races are always won by the current follower, i.e. the evolution of the market structure is characterised by Catching-Up.

---

[1] Hereafter with (CU2) we refer alternatively to both formulations of the condition.

[2] For simplicity $I(x,t)$ has been drawn as a linear function, although linearity is neither necessary nor assumed in our analysis.

5.4   Increasing Dominance

The analysis of Increasing Dominance has a similar structure to the one used for CU, so that we will be less detailed. We start from the last period, T. In T the leader wins the race if the following hold:

$$\pi\left(m_{T-1}+1,n_{T-1}\right)-\pi\left(m_{T-1},n_{T-1}+1\right)>\pi\left(n_{T-1}+1,m_{T-1}\right)-\pi\left(n_{T-1},m_{T-1}+1\right)$$
$$\textit{for } m_{T-1}>n_{T-1}$$

$$(5.17)$$

$$\pi\left(m_{T-1}+1,n_{T-1}\right)-\pi\left(m_{T-1},n_{T-1}+1\right)<\pi\left(n_{T-1}+1,m_{T-1}\right)-\pi\left(n_{T-1},m_{T-1}+1\right)$$
$$\textit{for } m_{T-1}<n_{T-1}$$

When $m_{T-1}=n_{T-1}$ random allocation occurs.

Moving back to period $t<T$ and assuming that ID prevails between t and T, we can write the conditions for ID as

$$\tau\left(m_{t-1}+1,n_{t-1}\right)>\tau\left(m_{t-1},n_{t-1}+1\right)\qquad\textit{for } m_{t-1}>n_{t-1}$$

$$(5.18)$$

$$\tau\left(m_{t-1}+1,n_{t-1}\right)<\tau\left(m_{t-1},n_{t-1}+1\right)\qquad\textit{for } m_{t-1}<n_{t-1}$$

As above, we concentrate on the case $m_{t-1}>n_{t-1}$. Thus (5.18) can be written as

$$\sigma\left(m_{t-1}+1,n_{t-1}\right)+\tau\left(m_{t-1}+2,n_{t-1}\right)-\left[\omega\left(n_{t-1}+1,m_{t-1}+1\right)-\omega\left(n_{t-1},m_{t-1}+2\right)\right]>$$
$$\sigma\left(m_{t-1},n_{t-1}+1\right)+\tau\left(m_{t-1}+1,n_{t-1}+1\right)-\left[\omega\left(n_{t-1}+2,m_{t-1}\right)-\omega\left(n_{t-1}+1,m_{t-1}+1\right)\right]$$

$$(5.19)$$

The assumption of ID prevailing in the continuation of the game implies that $\tau\left(m_{t-1}+2,n_{t-1}\right)>\tau\left(m_{t-1}+1,n_{t-1}+1\right)$. Then, the sufficient conditions on joint profit and next period's manager's price for ID are

$$\pi\left(m_{t-1}+1,n_{t-1}\right)-\pi\left(m_{t-1},n_{t-1}+1\right)>\pi\left(n_{t-1}+1,m_{t-1}\right)-\pi\left(n_{t-1},m_{t-1}+1\right)$$

$$(5.20)$$

and

$$\sum_{s=0}^{T-t-1}\left[\pi\left(n_{t-1}+2,m_{t-1}+s\right)-\pi\left(n_{t-1}+1,m_{t-1}+1+s\right)\right]>$$
$$\sum_{s=1}^{T-t}\left[\pi\left(n_{t-1}+1,m_{t-1}+s\right)-\pi\left(n_{t-1},m_{t-1}+1+s\right)\right]$$

$$(5.21)$$

Even with ID we have a set of two different conditions. Condition (5.20) refers to gross incentives, while (5.21) refers to the evolution of managers' prices.

By looking at (5.17), (5.20) and (5.21), we see that the conditions for ID depend on the shape of (5.16) as it was the case for CU; and again we can establish conditions on (5.16) for ID to prevail.

Lemma 5.4. Condition (5.21) is satisfied if

$I(x,t)$ is increasing in x for $x < (t-1)/2$. $\hspace{2cm}$ (ID1)

Proof. Again, note that $m_{t-1}>n_{t-1}$ implies $x<(t-1)/2$; the proof immediately follows.

Lemma 5.5. Condition (5.17) and (5.20) are satisfied if

$I(x, t) < I(t-1-x, t)$ for $x<(t-1)/2$. $\hspace{2cm}$ (ID2)

(ID2) is equivalent to the reverse of *H2* in Delbono (1989), that we write as (ID2')

$\sigma(m+1, n) > \sigma(m, n+1)$ for $m > n$. $\hspace{2cm}$ (ID2')

and it is the general condition for ID in his framework:[3] As we have done for CU, we sketch the two sufficient conditions for ID in Figure 5.2.

---

[3] As Delbono points out, his condition *H1* ($\pi(m, n) = 0$) is only a special case of the reverse of *H2*.

Figure 5.2: Conditions (ID1) and (ID2)

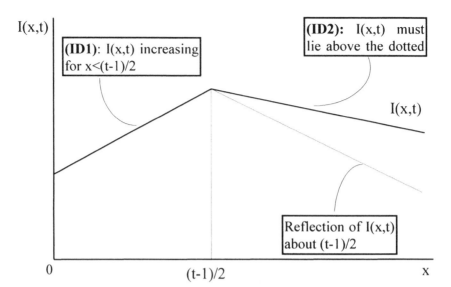

In the analysis of ID we do not need to worry much about the possibility of symmetric allocations, which are never reached in equilibrium and have an influence on the structure of incentives only when the game starts from an allocation of managers in which either $m_{t-1}=n_{t-1}+1$ or $m_{t-1}=n_{t-1}-1$. In that case, the price of the manager in period $t+1$ when firm B wins race t is determined by the difference between the sum of profits of being the winner or the loser in every period ever after. Therefore, (5.21) does not apply, since its left-hand side is replaced to get

$$\sum_{s=1}^{T-t}\left[\pi\left(n_{t-1}+1+s,m_{t-1}\right)-\pi\left(n_{t-1}+1,m_{t-1}+s\right)\right]>$$

$$\sum_{s=1}^{T-t}\left[\pi\left(n_{t-1}+1,m_{t-1}+s\right)-\pi\left(n_{t-1},m_{t-1}+1+s\right)\right]$$

$$for\ m_{t-1}>n_{t-1}\ and\ m_{t-1}=n_{t-1}+1 \tag{5.21a}$$

It is easy to see that this condition is satisfied whenever Lemmas 5.4 and 5.5 hold. [4]

---

[4] Note that, when $s=1$,

We can now summarise our results in the following proposition.

Proposition 5.6. If for $x < (t-1)/2$

i. function $I(x, t)$ is increasing in x

ii. $I(x, t) < I(t-1-x, t)$

then manager races are always won by the current leader, i.e. the evolution of the market structure is characterised by Increasing Dominance.

5.5   Market structure and returns to managers

We now proceed by looking at examples in which either CU or ID prevail. We concentrate on the effects of non-constant returns to managers on the evolution of market structure, i.e. we allow the change in unit costs deriving from the hiring of a new manager to vary with the number of managers a firm already has. We address this issue in a simple model of duopoly with quantity competition, linear demand and different degrees of independence among products' markets, so that we encompass the case of substitute, independent or complement products.

In this framework the inverse demand functions are given by

$$p_A = a - q_A - \gamma q_B \tag{5.22}$$

$$p_B = a - q_B - \gamma q_A \tag{5.22a}$$

$[\pi(n_{t-1}+1,m_{t-1}+s)-\pi(n_{t-1},m_{t-1}+1+s)]<[\pi(n_{t-1}+1+s,m_{t-1})-\pi(n_{t-1}+1,m_{t-1}+s)]$
for Lemma 5.4. When $s>1$
$[\pi(n_{t-1}+1,m_{t-1}+s)-\pi(n_{t-1},m_{t-1}+1+s)]<[\pi(n_{t-1}+2,m_{t-1}+s-1)-\pi(n_{t-1}+1,m_{t-1}+s)]$
for Lemma 5.4
$[\pi(n_{t-1}+2,m_{t-1}+s-1)-\pi(n_{t-1}+1,m_{t-1}+s)]<[\pi(m_{t-1}+s,n_{t-1})-\pi(m_{t-1}+s-1,n_{t-1}+2)]$
for Lemma 5.5, while it is always true that
$[\pi(m_{t-1}+s,n_{t-1}+1)-\pi(n_{t-1}+2,m_{t-1}+s-1)]<[\pi(n_{t-1}+1+s,m_{t-1})-\pi(n_{t-1}+1,m_{t-1}+s)].$
Therefore,
$[\pi(n_{t-1}+1,m_{t-1}+s)-\pi(n_{t-1},m_{t-1}+1+s)]<[\pi(n_{t-1}+1+s,m_{t-1})-\pi(n_{t-1}+1,m_{t-1}+s)].$

while the cost functions are those in equations (5.1) and (5.1a). Here $-1 \leq \gamma \leq 1$ represents the degree of interdependence between the two markets, which is a consequence of the degree of differentiation between products; in particular, we have perfect substitutes when $\gamma = 1$, independent products when $\gamma = 0$ and perfect complements when $\gamma = -1$.[5]

Straightforward calculations give us the profit functions:[6]

$$\pi_A = \left(\frac{2a - a\gamma + \gamma c_B(n) - 2c_A(m)}{4 - \gamma^2} \right)^2 \tag{5.23}$$

$$\pi_B = \left(\frac{2a - a\gamma + \gamma c_A(m) - 2c_B(n)}{4 - \gamma^2} \right)^2 \tag{5.23a}$$

We now provide formal definitions of what we mean by constant, decreasing and increasing returns to managers (CRM, DRM, IRM).

Definition 5.1 - Constant Returns to Managers (CRM). A production technology exhibits CRM when $c(x+2) - c(x+1) = c(x+1) - c(x)$ for all $x = m, n$.

Definition 5.2 - Decreasing Returns to Managers (DRM). A production technology exhibits DRM when $c(x) - c(x+1) > c(x+1) - c(x+2)$ for all $x = m, n$.

Definition 5.3 - Increasing Returns to Managers (IRM). A production technology exhibits IRM when $c(x) - c(x+1) < c(x+1) - c(x+2)$ for all $x = m, n$.

---

[5] However we will not investigate the market equilibrium for $\gamma = -1$, because it is well known that the maximisation problem of the consumer may not have a solution in that case, so that the demand is not defined.

[6] The corresponding equilibrium quantities are $q_A^* = \dfrac{a}{2\left(1 + \dfrac{\gamma}{2}\right)} + \dfrac{\gamma c(n) - 2c(m)}{4\left(1 - \dfrac{\gamma^2}{4}\right)}$ and

$q_B^* = \dfrac{a}{2\left(1 + \dfrac{\gamma}{2}\right)} + \dfrac{\gamma c(m) - 2c(n)}{4\left(1 - \dfrac{\gamma^2}{4}\right)}$.

We will also make the following convenient while not particularly restrictive assumptions.

Assumption 5.1 (on DRM). When a production technology exhibits DRM the following inequality holds:

$$[c(x)-c(x+1)]-[c(x+1)-c(x+2)]<[c(x-1)-c(x)]-[c(x)-c(x+1)]$$

for all $x=m,n$.

This implies that the reduction in production cost deriving from the acquisition of a new manager decreases at a declining rate as the number of managers increases.

Assumption 5.2 (on IRM). When a production technology exhibits IRM the following inequality holds:

$$[c(x)-c(x+1)]-[c(x+1)-c(x+2)]>[c(x-1)-c(x)]-[c(x)-c(x+1)]$$

for all $x=m,n$

This implies that the reduction in production cost deriving from the acquisition of a new manager increases at a decreasing rate as the number of managers increases.

Now we are ready to analyse the evolution of market structure in each of the three cases we have just presented. We will do that by trying to identify the circumstances under which the sufficient conditions for either CU or ID are satisfied. Throughout this section we assume that firm B is the leader, i.e. $m<n$.

5.5.1   Constant returns

We start from the simplest case of CRM. We check first for condition (ID2'). In the present case of linear duopoly the stage joint profit for constant as well as increasing and decreasing returns is:

$$\sigma(m,n)=\left[\frac{2}{\left(4-\gamma^2\right)^2}\right]\left[2a-a\gamma+\left(\frac{\gamma}{2}-1\right)(c(m)+c(n))\right]^2$$

$$+\left[\frac{2}{\left(4-\gamma^2\right)^2}\right]\left[\left(1+\frac{\gamma}{2}\right)(c(m)-c(n))\right]^2$$

(5.24)

We can establish the following lemma.

Lemma 5.7. When the technology exhibits CRM, (ID2') is always satisfied for any $-1 < \gamma \leq 1$.

Proof. We distinguish between two terms in (5.24), corresponding to two different effects on joint profit: an industry average cost term (IAC),

$$
\left[\frac{2}{\left(4 - \gamma^2\right)^2} \right] \left[2a - a\gamma + \left(\frac{\gamma}{2} - 1 \right)\left(c(m) + c(n)\right) \right]^2 , \text{ and a spread term}
$$

(S), $\left[\dfrac{2}{\left(4 - \gamma^2\right)^2} \right] \left[\left(1 + \dfrac{\gamma}{2} \right)\left(c(m) - c(n)\right) \right]^2$. For $m < n$, an increase in n

will make the spread term grow, while a rise of m would reduce it. By CRM, the industry average term will change by the same amount whichever is the winner. Therefore, the joint profit increases more when the leader wins the race than when the follower does. (QED)

We notice that, given Lemma 5.7, CU is ruled out with CRM. Hence, we inspect function $I(x,t)$ for the present case of linear duopoly to check whether (ID1) is also satisfied, so that ID prevails:

$$
I(x,t) = \left[\frac{2a - a\gamma + \gamma c(t - x - 1) - 2c(x + 1)}{4 - \gamma^2} \right]^2 - \left[\frac{2a - a\gamma + \gamma c(t - x) - 2c(x)}{4 - \gamma^2} \right]^2
$$

$$(5.25)$$

We can establish the following lemma.

Lemma 5.8. When the technology exhibits CRM, (ID1) is always satisfied for any $-1 < \gamma \leq 1$.

Proof. Let us consider the change in $I(x,t)$ due to an increase in x:

$$
\frac{\Delta I}{\Delta x} = I(x + 1, t) - I(x, t) = \frac{\Delta_2 \Psi_2 - \Delta_1 \Psi_1}{\left(4 - \gamma^2\right)^2}
$$

$$(5.26)$$

where

$$
\Delta_2 = \gamma \left[c(t - x - 2) - c(t - x - 1) \right] - 2\left[c(x + 2) - c(x + 1) \right]
$$

$$
\Delta_1 = \gamma \left[c(t - x - 1) - c(t - x) \right] - 2\left[c(x + 1) - c(x) \right]
$$

$$\Psi_2 = 4a - 2a\gamma + \gamma \left[c(t-x-2) + c(t-x-1) \right] - 2\left[c(x+2) + c(x+1) \right]$$

$$\Psi_1 = 4a - 2a\gamma + \gamma \left[c(t-x-1) + c(t-x) \right] - 2\left[c(x+1) + c(x) \right].$$

With CRM $\Delta_1 = \Delta_2 > 0$, while $\Psi_2 > \Psi_1 > 0$. Therefore, $\dfrac{\Delta I}{\Delta x} > 0$.

(QED).

We notice that the statements of both the lemmas in the present subsection are reinforced when γ increases. As far as Lemma 5.7 is concerned, a growth of γ increases the weight of the spread term in equation (5.24), which gets bigger as the leader gets more managers. As for lemma 5.8, a rise in γ increases the difference between Ψ_2 and Ψ_1.

Lemma 5.7 and 5.8 show that in the present framework, as in Delbono's, ID prevails in linear Cournot duopoly with CRM. The incentives for ID are stronger the larger is γ, i.e. the more the markets where the firms operate are interdependent.

5.5.2   Increasing returns

Let us now consider the case where a new manager produce larger efficiency gains if applied to more advanced technologies, i.e. the case of increasing returns to managers. In this case, on top of the effect on the spread term we saw for constant returns, an increase in the number of managers of the leader makes the industry average term increase more than a follower's victory. Hence we can state the following lemma.

Lemma 5.9. When the technology exhibits IRM, (ID2') is always satisfied for any $-1 < \gamma \le 1$.

Furthermore, an inspection of equation (5.26) allow us to state the following lemma.

Lemma 5.10. When the technology exhibits IRM, (ID1) is always satisfied for any $-1 < \gamma \le 1$.

Proof.

With IRM $\Delta_2 \ne \Delta_1$, and, in particular, it is always true that $\left[c(t-x-2) - c(t-x-1) \right] < \left[c(t-x-1) - c(t-x) \right]$ and $\left[c(x+2) - c(x+1) \right] < \left[c(x+1) - c(x) \right]$.

However, for Assumption 5.2 on IRM we know that for $x < t - x$

$$[c(x+2)-c(x+1)]-[c(x+1)-c(x)]<[c(t-x)-c(t-x-1)]-[c(t-x-1)-c(t-x-2)].$$

This implies $\Delta_2 > \Delta_1$ for any $\gamma \le 2$. Therefore, $\dfrac{\Delta I}{\Delta x} > 0$ for $x < t - x$, which implies (ID1). (QED)

Therefore, even with increasing returns ID prevails.

5.5.3   Decreasing returns

The case of decreasing returns is not clear-cut and we will see that both CU and ID might prevail. In this case the two effects on joint profit have opposite signs, because a leader's victory increases the spread term, but decreases the industry average cost term as a consequence of decreasing returns. Therefore, it cannot be generally established which is satisfied between (ID2') and (CU2').

Furthermore, by looking at $\dfrac{\Delta I}{\Delta x}$ we cannot generally establish whether (ID1) and (CU1) are satisfied or not for any $-1 < \gamma \le 1$. We know that in general $\Psi_2 > \Psi_1 > 0$, while with DRM $\Delta_2 \ne \Delta_1$.

In particular, $[c(t-x-2)-c(t-x-1)]>[c(t-x-1)-c(t-x)]$, while $[c(x+2)-c(x+1)]>[c(x+1)-c(x)]$. However, Assumption 5.1 implies $[c(x+2)-c(x+1)]-[c(x+1)-c(x)]>[c(t-x)-c(t-x-1)]-[c(t-x-1)-c(t-x-2)]$ when $x < t - x$. Then $\Delta_2 < \Delta_1$ for $x < t - x$. With $\Psi_2 > \Psi_1 > 0$ and $\Delta_2 < \Delta_1$ we cannot determine the sign of $\dfrac{\Delta I}{\Delta x}$ and, as a consequence, whether or not (ID1) is satisfied. Furthermore, we cannot establish in general whether (CU1) is satisfied with DRM, since for $x > t - x$,

$$[c(x+2)-c(x+1)]-[c(x+1)-c(x)]<[c(t-x)-c(t-x-1)]-[c(t-x-1)-c(t-x-2)]$$

so that we cannot tell which is larger between Δ_1 and Δ_2.

Therefore, with DRM we cannot generally predict whether or not a firm is able to relax competition in future races by letting the rival win. Indeed, given that also the analysis of gross incentives does not give general predictions, we cannot establish a prevalence of CU or ID as a pattern of market structure's evolution. However, it is important to note that, in contrast with what happens in Delbono (1989), in this framework CU is not ruled out in Cournot competition.

In the next section we will try to explore which features of the product market influence the evolution through further analytical discussion and some simulations.

5.6   Market size and product differentiation with DRM

In the previous section we have seen that one cannot tell in general whether the evolution of market's structure will be characterised by either CU or ID when DRM prevail. In this section we investigate how market size and product differentiation might affect the likelihood of either ID or CU prevailing. We analyse the influence of these characteristics of the market first on gross incentives and then on managers' prices. From that analysis we derive some quite clear, although not conclusive, indications on how market structure evolution would be affected. Subsequently, we consider the results of some numerical simulations, which appear to be consistent with the indications drawn from the analysis.

5.6.1   Gross incentives

We start by considering gross incentives to win manager races, which are expressed by the joint profit in equation (5.24). Throughout this section we assume that $m<n$.

A simple inspection of (5.24) shows that as γ decreases the gross incentives for CU (ID) grow (decline), since in the stage joint profit the weight of the Industry Average Cost term raises, while the weight of the Spread term reduces. Hence we can establish the following.

Lemma 5.11. The gross incentives for CU (ID) increase (decrease) as the degree of substitutability between the products of the two firms, γ, declines (raises).

The interpretation of this result is quite intuitive. As γ increases the two firms becomes more direct competitor, so that the negative cross effect on a firm profit of a reduction in the rival's unit cost becomes larger. Hence, as γ gets larger a potential follower's acquisition of a manager, which is more efficient in cost reducing than a leader's, becomes more effective in increasing the leader's incentives to win relatively to the extent by which it increases the follower's.

We proceed by comparing the gross incentives for CU, $\sigma(m+1,n)-\sigma(m,n)$, with the one for ID, $\sigma(n+1,m)-\sigma(n,m)$. It is easy to prove the following lemma.

Lemma 5.12. With DRM, $\sigma(n+1,m)-\sigma(n,m)>\sigma(m+1,n)-\sigma(m,n)$ if and only if

$$a<-\frac{\dfrac{\gamma}{2}-1}{2(2-\gamma)}\left[c(m)+c(m+1)+c(n)+c(n+1)\right]$$

$$-\frac{\left(1+\dfrac{\gamma}{2}\right)^2}{2(2-\gamma)\left(\dfrac{\gamma}{2}-1\right)}\frac{\left[c(m)-c(n+1)\right]^2-\left[c(m+1)-c(n)\right]^2}{c(m)+c(n+1)-c(n)-c(m+1)} \qquad (5.27)$$

Proof. Through straightforward algebra we calculate (5.27) by substituting (5.24), the extensive form for stage joint profit, in $\sigma(n+1,m)-\sigma(n,m)>\sigma(m+1,n)-\sigma(m,n)$. (QED)

Note that by DRM the right-hand side of (5.27) is positive, since the denominator of the last term is positive. Lemma 5.12 shows that the smaller is a the more likely it is that (ID2) be satisfied, while of course the opposite holds for (CU2). This happens because the size of the IAC effect is positively correlated with a, while the S effect is independent from a.

5.6.2   Managers' prices

We now consider the interaction between the evolution of managers' prices and market structure with DRM. In section 5.5 we have seen that with DRM $\dfrac{\Delta I}{\Delta x}$ cannot be unequivocally signed both when $x>t-x$, i.e. when we try to verify the condition on managers' prices for Increasing Dominance, and when $x<t-x$, i.e. when we do the same for Catching-Up.

However, the following lemmas provide conditions under which $\dfrac{\Delta I}{\Delta x}$ is positive and which in turn implies that either (ID1) or (CU1) are satisfied.[7]

Lemma 5.13. With DRM (CU1) is satisfied if

$$a > \frac{\{\gamma[c(m+1)-c(m+2)]+2[c(n)-c(n+1)]\}\{\gamma[c(m+1)+c(m+2)]-2[c(n)+c(n+1)]\}}{2(2-\gamma)\{\gamma[c(m)-c(m+1)]+2[c(n+1)-c(n+2)]-\gamma[c(m+1)-c(m+2)]-2[c(n)-c(n+1)]\}}$$

$$-\frac{\{\gamma[c(m)-c(m+1)]+2[c(n+1)-c(n+2)]\}\{\gamma[c(m)+c(m+1)]-2[c(n+2)+c(n+1)]\}}{2(2-\gamma)\{\gamma[c(m)-c(m+1)]+2[c(n+1)-c(n+2)]-\gamma[c(m+1)-c(m+2)]-2[c(n)-c(n+1)]\}}$$

(5.28a)

when the denominator of the two terms is positive or

$$a < \frac{\{\gamma[c(m+1)-c(m+2)]+2[c(n)-c(n+1)]\}\{\gamma[c(m+1)+c(m+2)]-2[c(n)+c(n+1)]\}}{2(2-\gamma)\{\gamma[c(m)-c(m+1)]+2[c(n+1)-c(n+2)]-\gamma[c(m+1)-c(m+2)]-2[c(n)-c(n+1)]\}}$$

$$-\frac{\{\gamma[c(m)-c(m+1)]+2[c(n+1)-c(n+2)]\}\{\gamma[c(m)+c(m+1)]-2[c(n+2)+c(n+1)]\}}{2(2-\gamma)\{\gamma[c(m)-c(m+1)]+2[c(n+1)-c(n+2)]-\gamma[c(m+1)-c(m+2)]-2[c(n)-c(n+1)]\}}$$

(5.28b)

when the denominator of the two terms is negative.

Proof. Direct from (5.26) for $x=n$ and $t-x-2=m$.

We note that when firm B's profit is positive the condition for the denominator to be positive, i.e.

$$\gamma[c(m)-c(m+1)]+2[c(n+1)-c(n+2)] > \gamma[c(m+1)-c(m+2)]+2[c(n)-c(n+1)]$$

(5.29)

implies that (CU1) is satisfied. This is easy to see if we consider the following

---

$$I(n+1,m+n+2)-I(n,m+n+2)=$$

$$\frac{1}{(4-\gamma^2)^2}\{[\gamma(c(m)-c(m+1))+2(c(n+1)-c(n+2))]$$

$$[2a(2-\gamma)+\gamma(c(m)+c(m+1))-2(c(n+1)+c(n+2))]+$$

$$-[\gamma(c(m+1)-c(m+2))+2(c(n)-c(n+1))]$$

$$[2a(2-\gamma)+\gamma(c(m+1)+c(m+2))-2(c(n)+c(n+1))]\}$$

(5.30)

and note that

$$[2a(2-\gamma)+\gamma(c(m)+c(m+1))-2(c(n+1)+c(n+2))]$$
$$>[2a(2-\gamma)+\gamma(c(m+1)+c(m+2))-2(c(n)+c(n+1))]\}$$

(5.31)

for DRM. Hence, it is more likely that (5.29) will be satisfied when the difference in the number of managers the two firms have gets larger. Therefore, when DRM holds and (5.29) is not satisfied (CU1) will be satisfied when either the difference in number of managers the firms have is sufficiently high or when a is sufficiently small.

We now consider the condition for price incentives for ID.

Lemma 5.14. With DRM (ID1) is satisfied if

$$a<\frac{\{\gamma[c(n+1)-c(n+2)]+2[c(m)-c(m+1)]\}\{\gamma[c(n+1)+c(n+2)]-2[c(m)+c(m+1)]\}}{2(2-\gamma)\{\gamma[c(n)-c(n+1)]+2[c(m+1)-c(m+2)]-\gamma[c(n+1)-c(n+2)]-2[c(m)-c(m+1)]\}}+$$
$$\frac{\{\gamma[c(n)-c(n+1)]+2[c(m+1)-c(m+2)]\}\{\gamma[c(n)+c(n+1)]-2[c(m+2)+c(m+1)]\}}{2(2-\gamma)\{\gamma[c(n)-c(n+1)]+2[c(m+1)-c(m+2)]-\gamma[c(n+1)-c(n+2)]-2[c(m)-c(m+1)]\}}$$

(5.32)

Proof. Similarly to the previous lemma, direct from (5.26) for $x=m$ and $t-x-2=n$.

We note that the denominator in (5.32) is always negative, since

$$[c(m)-c(m+1)]-[c(m+1)-c(m+2)]>[c(n)-c(n+1)]-[c(n+1)-c(n+2)]$$

for Assumption 5.1 on DRM, while the numerators are both negative and the first numerator is smaller than the second for similar reasons.

Therefore, the right hand side of condition (5.32) is always positive, so that the condition establishes an upper bound on a and (ID1) is satisfied when a is small enough. However, we note that there is also a lower bound on a, which guarantees that firm A makes a positive profit, i.e. for production to be profitable it must be that $a > \dfrac{2c(m) - \gamma c(n+2)}{(2-\gamma)}$. This can be easily derived from (5.23).

The effect of market size on manager prices incentives is not clear-cut. A large a favours CU if (5.29) is satisfied, but it discourages CU as well as ID otherwise. On the other hand very asymmetric allocation of managers tend to trigger CU in this respect.

Finally, we look at the effect of product differentiation on managers prices' incentives. Unfortunately, we are not able to determine unequivocally how changes in γ condition the satisfaction of (ID1) and (CU1).

The derivative of $I(m+1, m+n+2) - I(m, m+n+2)$ with respect to γ is

$$
\frac{d[I(m+1,t) - I(m,t)]}{d\gamma} = 4\gamma \left(4 - \gamma^2\right)^{-3} \left[I(m+1, m+n+2) - I(m, m+n+2) \right]
$$

$$
+ \left(4 - \gamma^2\right)^{-2} \left\{ [c(n) - c(n+1)][4a - 2a\gamma + \gamma(c(n) + c(n+1)) - 2(c(m+2) + c(m+1))] \right.
$$

$$
+ [\gamma(c(n) - c(n+1)) + 2(c(m+1) - c(m+2))][-2a + c(n) + c(n+1)]
$$

$$
- [c(n+1) - c(n+2)][4a - 2a\gamma + \gamma(c(n+1) + c(n+2)) - 2(c(m) + c(m+1))]
$$

$$
\left. - [\gamma(c(n+1) - c(n+2)) + 2(c(m) - c(m+1))][-2a + c(n+1) + c(n+2)] \right\}
$$

$$
\tag{5.33}
$$

The expression in curly brackets is positive for the first term is greater than the third and the second is greater than the fourth because of the assumption we have made on the cost function. However the sign of $4\gamma \left(4 - \gamma^2\right)^{-3} \left[I(m+1, m+n+2) - I(m, m+n+2) \right]$ is positive when

(ID1) is satisfied and negative otherwise. Hence, an increase in γ does not have an unequivocal effect on the satisfaction of (ID1), so that a higher substitutability between the products of firms A and B often but not always increases the managers prices incentives for ID.

The effect of γ on (CU1) cannot be generally established too. This can be seen by looking at the derivative of $I(n+1,n+m+2)-I(n,n+m+2)$ with respect to γ reported below,

$$\frac{d[I(n+1,t)-I(n,t)]}{d\gamma}=4\gamma\left(4-\gamma^2\right)^{-3}\left[I(n+1,n+m+2)-I(n,n+m+2)\right]$$

$$+4\gamma\left(4-\gamma^2\right)^{-2}\{[c(m)-c(m+1)][4a-2a\gamma+\gamma(c(m)+c(m+1))-2(c(n+2)+c(n+1))]$$
$$+[\gamma(c(m)-c(m+1))+2(c(n+1)-c(n+2))][-2a+c(m)+c(m+1)]$$
$$-[c(m+1)-c(m+2)][4a-2a\gamma+\gamma(c(m+1)+c(m+2))-2(c(n)+c(n+1))]$$
$$-[\gamma(c(m+1)-c(m+2))+2(c(n)-c(n+1))][-2a+c(m+1)+c(m+2)]\}$$

(5.34)

the first term has the same sign as $I(n+1,n+m+2)-I(n,n+m+2)$, while the first term in the curly brackets is larger than the third, but the second term may be greater or smaller than the fourth.

5.6.3   Simulations [8]

The analysis of the previous two subsections does not fully characterise the evolution of market structure with DRM. However, it does provide us with some important, although non-conclusive, indications on how the main features of the product market influence that evolution. Those indications may be summarised as follows.

1. Market size has a clear-cut first-order effect on gross incentives: gross incentives for CU are more likely to be larger than those for ID the larger is a. The effect of market size on the incentives connected to the evolution of managers' price is less clear-cut. However, the analysis shows that in this respect a large a does not favour ID. Therefore, we derive quite a

---

[8] The simulations, whose results are reported below, have been run using a program written in Pascal by Michael Luck of the Department of Computer Science, University of Warwick, and described in Appendix 5.1. His help is gratefully acknowledged.

strong indication that with DRM we are more likely to observe CU when the size of the market, a, is large with respect to the firms' size.

2. Product substitutability has a clear first order effect on gross incentives, since the larger is γ the more weight has the spread term in the joint profit function relative to the industry average cost term. On the other hand, the effect of γ on the incentives connected to managers' price is not generally clear both for ID and CU. One easy case is that in which (ID1) is satisfied: then an increase in γ makes it even more so. Therefore, a reasonable, although weaker than in the previous case, prediction on the effect of product substitutability on the evolution of market structure would be that an increase in γ supports ID.

In order to test these predictions we have run some simulations of the game, using the linear demand specification considered in the last two sections and the following specification for the cost function:

$$c_i = 1 + \frac{3}{x} \tag{5.35}$$

which satisfies the assumptions we made in section 5.5. Some results of the simulations with different values for a and γ are reported below. All the simulations start with both firms holding 1 manager. The first two columns of each table show the values of a and γ, the third the number of races we considered and the fourth the equilibrium pattern for the evolution of market structure.

Table 5.1 provides an overview of the results of the simulations. It shows that CU is the prevailing equilibrium pattern of market structure evolution in most of the possible market configuration when the number of races exceeds 10 or $a \geq 8$. However, ID is the equilibrium pattern in a not negligible number of cases.

Table 5.1: An overview of the simulations' results

MARKET SIZE a	DEGREE OF SUBSTITUTABILITY γ	NUMBER OF RACES n	EQUILIBRIUM PATTERN OF EVOLUTION
7	1	3	ID
7	1	10	ID
7	1	20	ID
8	1	3	ID
8	1	7	CU (after 1 ID round)
8	1	20	CU
9	1	3	ID
9	1	10	CU
9	1	20	CU
10	1	3	CU
10	1	10	CU
10	1	20	CU
7	0.8	3	ID
7	0.8	2	ID
8	0.8	2	ID
9	0.8	2	ID
10	0.8	2	CU
7	0.5	3	CU
7	0	3	CU
7	-0.5	3	CU
7	-1	3	CU

Table 5.2 shows that the number of cases when ID is the equilibrium pattern of evolution increases as the market's size relative to the firms' size gets smaller. This confirms the indication of the analysis and substatiates the intuition that an increase in the efficiency of the follower is less rewarded when the market is small than when it is large.

Table 5.2: Simulations' results: the effect of market's size

MARKET SIZE a	DEGREE OF SUBSTITUTABILITY γ	NUMBER OF RACES n	EQUILIBRIUM PATTERN OF EVOLUTION
7	1	3	ID
8	1	3	ID
9	1	3	ID
10	1	3	CU
7	1	20	ID
8	1	20	CU
9	1	20	CU
10	1	20	CU
7	0.8	2	ID
8	0.8	2	ID
9	0.8	2	ID
10	0.8	2	CU

Table 5.3 shows that the number of cases in which ID is the equilibrium pattern of evolution increases as the degree of substitutability between the two firms' products increases. Even in this respect the indications of the analysis is confirmed by the results of the simulations.

Table 5.3: Simulations' results: the effect of products substitutability

MARKET SIZE a	DEGREE OF SUBSTITUTABILITY γ	NUMBER OF RACES n	EQUILIBRIUM PATTERN OF EVOLUTION
7	1	3	ID
7	0.8	3	ID
7	0	3	CU
7	-0.8	3	CU
7	-1	3	CU

When the competition between the two firms becomes less fierceful, i.e. when their products become complementary or their degree of substitution decreases, the hiring of a new manager by a firm has a positive (or less negative) externality on the rival. Hence the incentive to win of the firm which has a smaller efficiency gain from the hiring of a new manager (i.e. the leader with DRM) gets smaller as the degree of substitutability between products reduces.

5.7   Some welfare implications

In the previous sections, we studied the market mechanism which allocates managers to firms. It has been shown that each manager is allocated to the firm that values it most. We now want to ascertain whether the equilibrium allocation is also socially efficient. As a measure of social welfare (SW) we take the sum of joint profit and consumer surplus (CS):

$$SW = \sigma(m,n) + CS \tag{5.36}$$

where CS is the sum of the consumer surpluses of the two markets:

$$CS = CS_A + CS_B \tag{5.37}$$

By using the linear demands in equations (5.22) and (5.22a), it is easy to calculate the following:

$$CS_A = \frac{(q_A + \gamma q_B)q_A}{2} \tag{5.38}$$

$$CS_B = \frac{(q_B + \gamma q_A)q_B}{2} \tag{5.39}$$

By substituting these and the equilibrium values for output in (5.37), we get

$$CS = \frac{1}{(4-\gamma^2)^2}\left[(2-\gamma)^2(1+\gamma)\left(a-\frac{c(m)+c(n)}{2}\right)^2 + \left(1-\frac{3\gamma^2}{4}-\frac{\gamma^3}{4}\right)(c(m)-c(n))^2\right] \tag{5.40}$$

For convenience we re-write here the expression for the stage joint profit:

$$\sigma(m,n)=\left[\frac{2}{\left(4-\gamma^2\right)^2}\right]\left[(2-\gamma)^2\left(a-\frac{c_A(m)+c_B(n)}{2}\right)^2\right]$$
$$+\left[\frac{2}{\left(4-\gamma^2\right)^2}\right]\left[\left(1+\frac{\gamma}{2}\right)(c_A(m)-c_B(n))\right]^2$$

(5.24)

We note that, like the expression for stage joint profit, also the aggregated CS has an Industry Average Cost term (IAC) and a Spread term (S). However, the relative weight of the two terms is different apart from the case of $\gamma = 0$, i.e. when the two product markets are perfectly independent. When $\gamma > 0$ IAC has more relative weight in CS than in σ, while S has more relative weight in CS than in σ when $\gamma < 0$. In particular, the consumer surplus is a direct increasing function of just the industry average cost with perfect substitute products ($\gamma = 1$) and of just the spread between costs with perfect complements ($\gamma = -1$).

By substituting (5.40) and (5.24) in (5.36) we get an expression for social welfare:

$$SW=\left[\frac{2}{\left(4-\gamma^2\right)^2}\right]\left[(2-\gamma)^2\left(a-\frac{c(m)+c(n)}{2}\right)^2\right]+\left[\frac{2}{\left(4-\gamma^2\right)^2}\right]\left[\left(1+\frac{\gamma}{2}\right)(c(m)-c(n))\right]^2+$$
$$+\frac{1}{\left(4-\gamma^2\right)^2}\left[(2-\gamma)^2(1+\gamma)\left(a-\frac{c(m)+c(n)}{2}\right)^2+\left(1-\frac{3\gamma^2}{4}-\frac{\gamma^3}{4}\right)(c(m)-c(n))^2\right]$$

(5.41)

A benevolent dictator would allocate the managers among firms in order to maximise the sum of the values of (5.41) for all the T periods. We note that the stage joint profits are both a determinant of market allocations and one of the two component of the measure of social welfare, while SW is not influenced by the prices paid for the managers, since in this framework prices are just transfers between different agents in the economy.[9] Therefore, the incentives determining the market allocation will differ from the objective of a benevolent dictator in two respects:

---

[9] Here we do not address the question of the incentives agents have for carrying out R&D activies.

i) the market allocation depends on managers' prices, while prices are irrelevant for social welfare;

ii) consumer surplus is a component of social welfare, but it does not influence market allocations.

In section 5.5 we have seen that the market allocation of managers will follow a pattern of Increasing Dominance both with IRM and CRM, since in both cases (ID1) and (ID2) are satisfied. A quick inspection of (5.41) show us that also social welfare is maximised by ID in these two regimes of returns to managers. The Spread terms increase when the leader wins and decrease when the follower wins; the Industry Average Cost terms increase by the same extent whichever is the winner with CRM and increase more with a leader's victory with IRM. Hence we can state the following proposition.

Proposition 5.15. With CRM and IRM the market allocation of managers maximises social welfare.

Then, we consider DRM and in particular the case when CU prevails and (CU2) is satisfied and the case when ID prevails and (ID2) is satisfied.

a. CU prevails with (CU2) satisfied.

As we noted above, the relative weight of IAC with respect to S is larger in the CS than in the joint profit when $\gamma > 0$, is equal when $\gamma = 0$ and is smaller when $\gamma < 0$.

As it is well known and can be seen from (5.38) and (5.39), when the firms' unit costs are equal CS converges towards 0 as γ converges towards -1. Hence, when products are (almost) perfect complements the firms capture (almost) all the consumer surplus. More generally, the firms are able to exploit any degree of products' complementarity to increase the equilibrium prices and capture some of the consumers' utility. The capability of doing so is at a maximum when the production costs are equal for the two products. This happens because the price of the leader's product, i.e. the product with the larger equilibrium output, decreases as the difference between the production costs of the two firms increases, and that reduction more than offsets the opposite effect on the price of the follower's product.

Therefore, in this case when $\gamma \geq 0$ a round of CU always increases SW more than a round of ID, while the effect is ambiguous when $\gamma < 0$, since CS is reduced by CU.

We can now state the following lemma.

Lemma 5.16. With DRM when (CU2) is satisfied and $\gamma \geq 0$, CU, the market equilibrium, is socially optimum. When $\gamma < 0$ CU may be socially inefficient.

Although possible in principle, the distortion in social efficiency referred to in Lemma 5.16 does not seem to be likely to happen and we are not able to provide examples for that in our simulations.

<u>b. ID prevails with (ID2) satisfied</u>

For the same kind of reasoning as above, when $\gamma \leq 0$ ID increases social welfare more than CU, while the opposite may hold when $\gamma > 0$. We can state the following lemma.

Lemma 5.17. With DRM, when (ID2) is satisfied and $\gamma \leq 0$ ID, the market equilibrium, is socially optimum, while it may be socially inefficient when $\gamma > 0$.

In this case we can show some examples of an equilibrium pattern of evolution which is not socially efficient. We have run simulations to establish the social welfare maximising pattern of evolution.[10]

In Table 5.4 the results of these simulations are compared with some of the results shown above. We note that with perfect substitute products in many cases the market evolution follows a socially inefficient pattern, since ID prevails when CU is socially desirable.

---

[10] These simulations have been run using a slightly modified version of the program used for the simulations whose results are reported in section 5.6. Also this program is reported in Appendix 5.1. The help of Michael Luck is gratefully acknowledged also in this case.

Table 5.4: Simulations' results: social welfare

MARKET SIZE	DEGREE OF SUBSTITUTA- BILITY	NUMBER OF RACES	EQUILIBRIUM PATTERN OF EVOLUTION	WELFARE MAX. PATTERN OF EVOLUTION
a	γ	n		
7	1	3	ID	CU (after 1 ID round)
7	1	10	ID	CU (after 1 ID round)
7	1	20	ID	CU (after 1 ID round)
8	1	3	ID	CU
8	1	6	ID	CU
8	1	20	CU	CU
9	1	3	ID	CU
9	1	10	CU	CU
10	1	10	CU	CU

In this section, we have shown that with DRM the market allocation of managers may be socially inefficient. In particular, when the products of the two firms are substitute ID may be socially undesirable, while CU may be socially undesirable with complementary products. When the products are substitute, consumers benefit from the production costs of the two firms being similar, because this ensures a more fierceful competition between them and so lower prices. This contrasts with the desire of the market leader to increase its dominance and with its ability to attain that in equilibrium. On the other hand, when the products are complementary consumers benefit from the production costs of the two firms being different, because this keeps low the price of the product they buy more. This contrasts with the follower's objective to catch up and with this capability to do so in equilibrium.

There are no obvious policy instruments to correct these distortions. A subsidy for R&D activities evenly distributed among firms, which is sometimes advocated for, would not change the structure of incentives for winning the races, since those incentives are all expressed in terms of differences between winning and losing, so that the subsidies would cancel out. The introduction of a selective subsidy for the firm whose victory is socially desirable makes it necessary to extract from firms information about their own costs, which in general they will not be prepared to reveal truthfully.

5.8   Conclusions

In this chapter we have studied the evolution of duopoly, when the market structure is influenced by a sequence of competitions between firms to acquire new managers, which we call "manager races". I applied to this problem and extended an analysis by Delbono (1989), whose main focus was the formally similar issue of sequence of patent races. I have considered a more general setting, which allows for prices paid for managers to be competitively set and the technology to be characterised by non-constant returns to managers. I have shown that the pattern of evolution, in this setting, is determined by two different factors, both belonging to the incentive for acquiring a new manager known in the literature of patent races as "competitive threat": the continuation payoffs gross of managers' prices, which the winner of the race attains, and the influence that the outcome of the current race has on future managers' prices. While the former factor had already been recognised in the literature, the analysis of the latter has not been carried out in detail before, since that factor does not play a crucial role in leap-frog models, which prevail in the literature on sequence of innovations, while it is not discussed in Delbono (1989) for the role played by participation costs in his model. By losing the current race a firm might be able to relax competition in future races and, through that, increase its overall payoff. In section 3 and 4 I prove sufficient conditions for Catching-Up and Increasing Dominance for our more general setting.

In section 5 I have applied those conditions to the case of linear Cournot duopoly with potentially differentiated products. I have shown that Increasing Dominance always prevails with both constant and increasing returns to managers, while the outcome of the market evolution with decreasing returns cannot be established in general. In this framework, at difference with what happens in Delbono (1989), one can have Catching-Up also in a Cournot duopoly: a market leader may lose the competition for the acquisition of a new manager, while retaining the market leadership. This proposition is substantiated in section 5.6 through some numerical simulations that show CU prevailing as the equilibrium pattern of evolution in many different settings.

Both the analysis of gross incentives and simulations show that Increasing Dominance becomes more frequent as the degree of substitutability between products increases and the market size decreases. High substitutability between products implies larger cross-effects of cost reductions on rival's profit: the potential follower's efficiency gains, larger than the leader's, have a larger positive effect on the leader's incentives to win the races. On the other hand, an efficiency gain of the follower is less rewarded when the market size is small. Furthermore, I have shown that the equilibrium pattern of evolution may be socially inefficient. In particular, we provide some numerical examples of ID prevailing while not being socially optimal in small sized markets with highly substitutable products.

Therefore, small and very competitive markets tend to favour the accumulation of managers in a single, increasingly dominant firm. This equilibrium pattern of evolution certainly hurts consumers, as it is most intuitive, but it is also socially inefficient in many cases. Larger sized markets, with more differentiated products, give a better deal to consumers and seem to ensure a socially efficient evolution in the distribution of human resources between firms.

In previous chapters, I have shown that the social welfare effect of strategic delegation in firms in a static framework is uncertain. The analysis of the present chapter shows that also the dynamic competition for delegates may deliver a socially inefficient outcome.

Appendix 5.1 - Programs for the simulations

The two programs used for the simulations whose results are discussed in sections 7 and 8 are reported below.

The first one was used to calculate the equilibrium pattern of evolution of market structure. Here there is its version for $\gamma = 1$. The function "pippo" in the program is the profit function, while functions "sigval" and "tauval" are the values for the joint profit (function σ) and for the joint continuation payoff (function τ); ca $:= 1 + (3/x)$ and cb $:= 1 + (3/y)$ are of course the cost functions for firm A and B.

Program A5.1.1 - Equilibrium Pattern of Evolution

```
program stuff (input,output);
{const aconst = 10;                    constant for pi formula}
    {depth = 8;           depth of the graph}
type ptr = ^tnode;                         {pointer to a tree}
    tnode = record
            na: integer;
            nb: integer;
            sigval : real;
            tauval: real;
            pippoval: real;
            upnode: ptr;
            dnnode: ptr;
        end;
var inita, initb: integer;
    temp, head: ptr;
    first: boolean;
    aconst: real;
    depth: integer;
function pippo (x,y: integer): real;
  var ca, cb: real;
  begin
   ca := 1 + (3/x);
   cb := 1 + (3/y);
   pippo := sqr((aconst - (2*ca) + cb)/3)
  end;
function sigma (na, nb: integer): real;
  begin
   sigma := pippo(na,nb) + pippo(nb,na)
  end;
function max (x,y: real): real;
begin
  if x < y then max := y
  else max := x
end;
procedure makenode (var this,prev: ptr;
                  newna,newnb: integer;
                  level: integer);
begin
  if level >0 then
```

```
  begin
    this^.na := newna;
    this^.nb := newnb;
    this^.sigval := sigma(this^.na,this^.nb);
    this^.pippoval := pippo(this^.na,this^.nb);
      if not first then
      this^.upnode := prev^.upnode^.dnnode
    else
      begin
        new(this^.upnode);
        makenode(this^.upnode, this, this^.na+1, this^.nb, level-1)
      end;
      new(this^.dnnode);
    makenode(this^.dnnode, this, this^.na, this^.nb+1, level-1);
    this^.tauval := this^.sigval + max (
              (this^.dnnode^.tauval -
              (this^.upnode^.pippoval-this^.dnnode^.pippoval)),
              (this^.upnode^.tauval -
              (pippo(this^.nb+1,this^.na)-pippo(this^.nb,this^.na+1)))):
    write('node ',newna:3, newnb:3, this^.sigval:8:4);
    writeln('tauval: ',this^.tauval:6:4);
    end
  else
    begin
      first := false;
      this^.upnode := nil;
      this^.dnnode := nil;
      this^.na := 0;
      this^.nb := 0;
      this^.sigval := 0;
      this^.pippoval := 0;
      this^.tauval := this^.sigval
    end
end;
begin
  writeln('Type the initial values for na and nb: ');
  readln(inita, initb);
  writeln('Type the value for the constant parameter a: ');
  readln(aconst);
  writeln('Type the value for the depth: ');
  readln(depth);
```

```
new(head);
head^.na := inita;
head^.nb := initb;
head^.sigval := sigma(head^.na, head^.nb);
first := true;
new(head^.upnode); new(head^.dnnode);
makenode(head^.upnode, head, inita+1, initb, depth-1);
makenode(head^.dnnode, head, inita, initb+1, depth-1);
writeln;
writeln('Optimum Path:');
temp := head;
{ writeln ('node ',temp^.na:1, temp^.nb:1, 'tauval: ',temp^.tauval:6:4);}
 while temp^.upnode <> nil do
   begin
    if temp^.upnode^.tauval > temp^.dnnode^.tauval then
     temp := temp^.upnode
    else
     temp := temp^.dnnode;
    writeln ('node ',temp^.na:1, temp^.nb:1, 'tauval: ',temp^.tauval:6:4);
   end;
end.
```

The second program was used to calculate the social welfare maximising pattern. Here there is its version for $\gamma = 1$. This program differs from Program A5.1.1 in two main respects. First function pippo is no longer the profit function, but is written in a way so that sigval becomes the value of social welfare in any period. Furthermore, tauval does no longer take into account the patents' prices, so that it becomes the continuation value for social welfare.

Program A5.1.2 - Social Welfare Maximising Pattern of Evolution

```
program stuff (input,output);
{const aconst = 10;              constant for pi formula}
    {depth = 8;          depth of the graph}
type ptr = ^tnode;                  {pointer to a tree}
   tnode = record
           na: integer;
           nb: integer;
           sigval : real;
           tauval: real;
```

```
            pippoval: real;
            upnode: ptr;
            dnnode: ptr;
          end;
var inita, initb: integer;
    temp, head: ptr;
    first: boolean;
    aconst: real;
    depth: integer;
function pippo (x,y: integer): real;
  var ca, cb: real;
  begin
    ca := 1 + (3/x);
    cb := 1 + (3/y);
    pippo := sqr((aconst - (2*ca) + cb)/3) - (1/8)*sqr(ca-cb)
  end;
function sigma (na, nb: integer): real;
  begin
    sigma := 2*(pippo(na,nb) + pippo(nb,na))
  end;
function max (x,y: real): real;
begin
  if x < y then max := y
  else max := x
end;
procedure makenode (var this,prev: ptr;
                    newna,newnb: integer;
                    level: integer);
begin
  if level >0 then
    begin
      this^.na := newna;
      this^.nb := newnb;
      this^.sigval := sigma(this^.na,this^.nb);
      this^.pippoval := pippo(this^.na,this^.nb);
        if not first then
        this^.upnode := prev^.upnode^.dnnode
      else
        begin
        new(this^.upnode);
        makenode(this^.upnode, this, this^.na+1, this^.nb, level-1)
```

```
      end;
      new(this^.dnnode);
    makenode(this^.dnnode, this, this^.na, this^.nb+1, level-1);
    this^.tauval := this^.sigval + max (
              (this^.dnnode^.tauval),
              (this^.upnode^.tauval));
    write('node ',newna:3, newnb:3, this^.sigval:8:4);
    writeln('tauval: ',this^.tauval:6:4);
  end
 else
   begin
    first := false;
    this^.upnode := nil;
    this^.dnnode := nil;
    this^.na := 0;
    this^.nb := 0;
    this^.sigval := 0;
    this^.pippoval := 0;
    this^.tauval := this^.sigval
   end
end;
begin
  writeln('Type the initial values for na and nb: ');
  readln(inita, initb);
  writeln('Type the value for the constant parameter a: ');
  readln(aconst);
  writeln('Type the value for the depth: ');
  readln(depth);
  new(head);
  head^.na := inita;
  head^.nb := initb;
  head^.sigval := sigma(head^.na, head^.nb);
  first := true;
  new(head^.upnode); new(head^.dnnode);
  makenode(head^.upnode, head, inita+1, initb, depth-1);
  makenode(head^.dnnode, head, inita, initb+1, depth-1);
  writeln;
  writeln('Optimum Path:');
  temp := head;
{  writeln ('node ',temp^.na:1, temp^.nb:1, 'tauval: ',temp^.tauval:6:4);}
  while temp^.upnode <> nil do
```

```
     begin
       if temp^.upnode^.tauval > temp^.dnnode^.tauval then
         temp := temp^.upnode
       else
         temp := temp^.dnnode;
       writeln ('node ',temp^.na:1, temp^.nb:1, 'tauval: ',temp^.tauval:6:4);
       end;
   end.
```

Chapter 6 - Conclusions

In this book I have attempted to contribute to our understanding of the phenomenon of strategic delegation, with particular reference to the organisation of firms and of the trade union, and to its welfare implications. I have discussed how different market and non-market relations involving delegates connect to each other. In chapters 2 and 3 I have considered how the need to delegate decisions concerning the product market to managers, and to compensate them through incentive contracts, modifies firms' strategy space and allows them to attain equilibria that are different from the one which would have been reached were the owners directly playing the product market game.

In chapter 2 it has been shown that in a Cournot duopoly played through managers, owners are able to use delegation strategically by making managerial incentive contracts observable even if the product market game is played under incomplete information on the rival's marginal cost. In equilibrium, managers' effort, which is assumed to decrease the expected value of marginal cost, will be higher than without strategic delegation. The observability of the incentive contract is used to inform the rival firm of a strategic reduction of marginal cost, which is not directly observable. We modelled the relation between owners and managers as being characterised by moral hazard. When moral hazard implies under-provision of effort, strategic delegation at least partially compensates that distortion. An increase in the level of competition in the product market, obtained by preventing firms from colluding, is shown to have a similar effect in reducing agency costs. Finally, in this setting strategic delegation may not be advantageous for consumers, since the equilibrium price is distorted towards monopoly price in each state of nature, although good states become more likely.

Chapter 3 contains two slightly different models of delegation in Cournot duopoly with settings similar to the one of chapter 2: owners select managerial incentive contracts, while managers play the product market game. It has been shown that observable but renegotiable contracts can be used by owners to co-ordinate in order to implement any product market equilibrium allowing the owners to get a level of profit at least as large as the profit obtainable in the strategic delegation equilibrium without renegotiations, which is used as a threat point. The equilibrium set includes joint profit maximisation, that is, perfect collusion. These Folk Theorem-like results are derived both when only one round of perfectly observable renegotiations is allowed and when renegotiations only becomes observable to rivals with a short delay, while renegotiations are costly.

The models of chapters 2 and 3 are both extensions of the previous literature on delegation in oligopoly. The analysis of chapter 2 shows that the standard results of strategic delegation are still valid when the product market game is played under incomplete information, while the equilibrium may not be as favourable to consumers as the corresponding equilibrium under complete information. The analysis of chapter 3 takes the assumption of contract observability to its extreme consequences, showing that delegation can be used to support a very large set of different equilibria, many of which are harmful to consumers. More generally, this analysis suggests a cautious assessment of the results of any strategic delegation model based on contracts that are not renegotiation-proof.

In chapter 4 I have studied the strategic delegation of authority in the trade union, and, in particular, how the union can be represented as a political institution where the authority is delegated to a leader. I have shown that workers can find it profitable to delegate to a professional leader, who does not need to bear the costs of industrial actions. This allows to credibly committing to implement threats that are at the same time effective but costly for the workers. The equilibrium wage and the number of employed workers will be larger under a professional leadership, so that this organisational setting may turn out to be both privately optimal for workers and social welfare maximising.

Therefore, strategic delegation turns out to be a useful mean to increase organisation effectiveness in the trade union as well as in firms.

In chapter 5 I have considered the evolution of market structure when firms compete for the acquisition of managers, and the effect on costs of the manager's acquisition depends on previous history. I have derived general sufficient conditions for the pattern of evolution of market structure to be characterised by Increasing Dominance and Catching-Up. I have extended previous analyses to consider the case when returns to managers may be non-constant. The equilibrium pattern of evolution, when firms compete *à la Cournot* in the product market, turns out to be Increasing Dominance both with constant and increasing returns to managers. However, Catching-Up may occur with decreasing returns. Comparative statics and some simulation results derived for this case show that Catching-Up becomes less likely as the degree of substitutability between firms' products increases and the market size decreases. Of course, the opposite holds for Increasing Dominance. It is also shown that with decreasing returns Increasing Dominance might prevail, while not being socially desirable. Therefore, in very competitive and small product markets, increasingly dominant firms tend to accumulate human capital in a way that hurts consumers and may not be socially efficient. Larger markets, with more differentiated products, favour consumers and in many cases ensure a socially efficient evolution of the distribution of managerial skills.

Strategic delegation is a widespread phenomenon in economic and social systems. It has been studied extensively in the literature, in particular with reference to firms' behaviour and central banks independence. This book is an attempt to highlight some further distinctive features of such phenomenon: extending the analysis of its implications for firms' strategy in product markets, investigating how it may affect the trade union's activity, studying its dynamic influence on the evolution of strategic interactions that the delegating party is involved in.

The welfare assessments of strategic delegation in the different settings I have considered are not unanimous. This suggests that policy interventions on such matter might be useful in some circumstances, but has to be evaluated and designed on a case by case basis. As it is often the case, the theoretical analysis helps to improve our understanding of the main forces behind economic phenomena, but it does not deliver ready-to-use and universal recipe for policy design.

References

Arrow, K.J. (1962) "Economic welfare and the allocation of resources to inventions", in Nelson, R. (ed.), *The Rate and Direction of Incentive Activity*, Princeton, Princeton University Press.

Basu, K. (1990) "Duopoly Equilibria when Firms can Change their Decision Once", *Economics Letters*, vol.32, pp.273-275.

Basu, K. (1995) "Stackelberg equilibrium in oligopoly: an explanation based on managerial incentives", *Economics Letters*, vol.49, pp.459-464.

Baye, M. (2000) ed. "*Advances in Applied Microeconomics. Vol. 9: Industrial Organisation*", Amsterdam - New York, Jai Press-Elsevier Science.

Beath, J., Y. Katsoulacos and D. Ulph (1995) "Game-Theoretic Approaches to the Modelling of Technological Change", in Stoneman, P. (ed.) *Handbook of the Economics of Innovation and Technological Change*, Oxford, Basil Blackwell.

Beath, J., Y. Katsoulacos and D. Ulph (1987) "Sequential Product Innovation and Industry Evolution", *The Economic Journal,* vol. 97, pp.32-43.

Bertoletti P. and C. Poletti (1996) "A Note on Endogenous Firm Efficiency in Cournot Models of Incomplete Information", *Journal of Economic Theory*, vol.71, pp.303-310.

Brander, J. and B. Spencer (1983) "Strategic Commitment with R&D: The Symmetric Case, *The Bell Journal of Economics*, vol.14, pp.225-235.

Budd, C., C. Harris and J. Vickers (1993) "A Model of the Evolution of Duopoly: Does the Asymmetry between Firms Tend to Increase or Decrease?", *Review of Economic Studies,* vol.60, pp. 543-573.

Bulow, J., J. Geanakoplos and P.Klemperer (1985) "Holding Idle Capacity to Deter Entry", *The Economic Journal*, vol.95, pp.178-182.

Caillaud, B., B. Jullien and P. Picard (1995) "Competing Vertical Structures: Pre-commitment and Renegotiation", *Econometrica*, vol. 63, pp. 621-646.

Chakrabarti, S. (1990) "Characterizations of the Equilibrium Payoffs of Inertia Supergames", *Journal of Economic Theory,* vol.51, pp.171-183.

Coase R.H. (1937), The Nature of the Firm, *Economica*, vol.4, n.15, pp.386-405.

Dasgupta, P. and J. Stiglitz (1980) "Industrial structure and the nature of innovative activity", *The Economic Journal*, vol.90, pp.266-293.

Delbono, F. (1989) "Market Leadership with a Sequence of History Dependent Patent Races", *The Journal of Industrial Economics,* vol.38, pp.95-101.

Dewatripont, M. (1988) "Commitment Through Renegotiation-Proof Contracts with Third Parties". *Review of Economic Studies*, vol.55, pp.377-390.

Dixit, A. (1980) "The Role of Investment in Entry Deterrence", *The Economic Journal*, vol.90, pp.95-106.

Dunlop J.T. (1944), *Wage Determination under Trade Unions*, New York, MacMillan.

Faith R.L. and J.D. Reid (1987), An Agency Theory of Unionism, *Journal of Economic Behaviour and Organisation*, vol.8, n.1, pp.39-60.

Fershtman, C. and K. Judd (1987) "Equilibrium Incentives in Oligopoly", *American Economic Review*, vol.77, pp.927-940.

Fershtman, C., K. Judd and E. Kalai (1991) "Observable Contracts: Strategic Delegation and Co-operation", *International Economic Review*, vol.32, no.3, pp.551-559.

Fudenberg, D. and J. Tirole (1983) "Learning by Doing and Market Performance", *The Bell Journal of Economics*, vol.14, pp.522-530.

Fudenberg, D. and J. Tirole (1984) "The Fat Cat Effect, the Puppy Dog Ploy and the Lean and Hungry Look", *American Economic Review*, Papers and Proceedings, vol. 74, pp.361-368.

Gatsios, K. and L. Karp (1991) "Delegation games in Customs Unions", *Review of Economic Studies*, vol.58, pp.391-397.

Grossman S. and O. Hart (1986), The Cost and Benefits of Ownership: A Theory of Vertical and Lateral Integration, *Journal of Political Economy*, vol.94, n.4, pp.691-719.

Grossman, S.J. and O.D. Hart (1983) "An Analysis of the Principal-Agent Problem", *Econometrica*, vol. 51, no. 1, pp.7-45.

Harris, C. and J. Vickers (1987) "Racing with Uncertainty", *Review of Economic Studies*, vol.54, p.1-21.

Hart O. and J. Moore (1990), Property Rights and the Nature of the Firm, *Journal of Political Economy*, vol.98, n.6, pp.1119-1158.

Hart, O. (1983) "The market mechanism as an incentive scheme", *The Bell Journal of Economics*, vol.14, pp.366-382.

Hart, O. and B. Holmstrom (1987) "The Theory of Contracts", in *Advances in Economic Theory*, Bewley, T. ed.

Hermalin, B. (1992) "The effects of competition on executive behavior", *Rand Journal of Economics*, vol.23, pp.350-365.

Hoel M. (1987), Bargaining Games with a Random Sequence of Who Makes the Offers, *Economics Letters*, vol. 24, n.1, pp.5-9.

Holmstrom, B. (1979) "Moral Hazard and Observability", *The Bell Journal of Economics*, vol. 10, pp.74-91.

Jewitt, I. (1988) "Justifying the First-Order Approach to Principal-Agent Problems", *Econometrica*, vol. 56, no. 5, pp.1177-1190.

Katz, M. (1991) "Game-playing agents: unobservable contracts as pre-commitments", *Rand Journal of Economics*, vol.22, no.3, pp.307-328.

Kreps, D.M. (1990) "*A Course in Microeconomic Theory*". New York, Harvester Wheatsheaf.

Lohmann, S. (1992) "Optimal Commitment in Monetary Policy", *American Economic Review*, vol.82, pp.273-286.

MacDonald I.M. and R.M. Solow (1981), Wage Bargaining and Employment, *American Economic Review*, vol.71, n.5, pp.896-908.

Macho-Stadler, I. and T. Verdier (1991) "Strategic Managerial Incentives and Cross Ownership Structure: A Note", *Journal of Economics*, vol.53, no.3, pp.285-297.

Martin S. (1993) "Endogenous Firm Efficiency in a Cournot Principal-Agent Model", *Journal of Economic Theory*, vol.59, pp.445-450.

McCutcheon, B. (1997), "Do Meetings in Smoke-Filled Rooms Facilitate Collusion?". *Journal of Political Economy*, vol.105, pp.330-350.

Melumad N.D. and D. Mookherjee (1989), Delegation as commitment: the case of income tax audits, *Rand Journal of Economics*, vol.20, n.2, pp.139-163.

Merzoni, G. (1991) "Qualità dei managers e incentivi in un modello di duopolio con separazione tra proprietà e controllo.", *Annali della Fondazione Einaudi - Torino*, vol.25, pp.137-159.

Milgrom P. and J. Roberts (1990), Bargaining costs, influence costs, and the organization of economic activity, in J.E. Alt e K.A. Shepsle (a cura di), *Perspectives on Positive Political Economy*, Cambridge, Cambridge University Press, pp.57-89.

Mirrlees, J.A. (1975) "The Theory of Moral Hazard and Unobservable Behaviour - Part I", Nuffield College, Oxford, mimeo. Published in 1999 on the *Review of Economic Studies*, vol. 66, n. 1, pp.3-21.

Moene K.O. (1988), Union Threats and Wage Determination, *The Economic Journal*, vol.98, n.391, pp.471-483.

Muthoo A. (1992), Revocable Commitment and Sequential Bargaining, *The Economic Journal*, vol.102, n.411, pp.378-387.

Myerson R. (1991), *Game Theory. Analysis of Conflict*, Cambridge, Mass., Harvard University Press.

Osborne M.J. and A. Rubinstein (1990), *Bargaining and Markets*, San Diego, Academic Press.

Oswald A.J. (1985), The economic theory of trade unions: an introductory survey, *Scandinavian Journal of Economics*, vol.87, n.2, pp.160-193.

Pal, D. (1991) "Cournot Duopoly with Two Production Periods and Cost Differentials", *Journal of Economic Theory*, vol.55, pp.441-448.

Pemberton J. (1988), A Managerial Model of the Trade Union, *The Economic Journal*, vol.98, n.392, pp.755-771.

Persson, T. and G. Tabellini (1997) "Designing Institutions for Monetary Stability", *Carnegie Rochester Conference Series on Public Policy*, vol. 39, pp.53-84.

Polo, M. and P. Tedeschi (1997) "Equilibrium and Renegotiation in Delegation Games", *IGIER-Bocconi Working Paper* n. 116.

Reinganum, J.F. (1985) "Innovation and Industry Evolution", *Quarterly Journal of Economics,* vol.99, pp.81-99.

Rogoff K. (1985), The Optimal Degree of Commitment to an Intermediate Monetary Target, *Quarterly Journal of Economics*, vol.100, n.4, pp.1169-1190.

Ross A. (1948), *Trade Union Wages Policy*, Berkeley, California University Press.

Rubinstein A. (1982), Perfect Equilibrium in a Bargaining Model, *Econometrica*, vol.50, n.1, pp.97-109.

Saloner, G. (1987) "Cournot Duopoly with Two Production Periods", *Journal of Economic Theory*, vol.42, pp.183-187.

Scharfstein, D. (1988) "Product-market competition and managerial slack", *Rand Journal of Economics*, vol.19, pp.147-155.

Schelling, T.C. (1960) *"The Strategy of Conflict"*. Cambridge, Mass. Harvard University Press.

Schmalensee, R. (1983) "Advertising and Entry Deterrence: An Exploratory Model", *Journal of Political Economy*, vol.90, pp.636-653.

Sklivas, S.D. (1987) "The Strategic Choice of Management Incentives", *Rand Journal of Economics*, vol.18, pp.452-458.

Spence, A.M. (1977) "Entry, Capacity, Investment and Oligopolistic Pricing", *The Bell Journal of Economics*, vol.8, pp.534-544.

Vickers, J. (1985) "Delegation and the theory of the firm", *The Economic Journal, Supplement*, vol.53, pp.138-147.

Vickers, J. (1986), "The Evolution of Market Structure when there is a Sequence of Innovations", *The Journal of Industrial Economics,* vol.35, pp.1-12.

von Stackelberg, H. (1934) *Marktform und Gleichgewicht*. Vienna, Julius Springer.

Walsh, C.E. (1995) "Optimal Contracts for Central Bankers", *American Economic review*, vol. 85, pp.150-167.

Williamson O. (1986), Economic Organization. Firms, Markets and Policy Control, Wheatsheaf Books.

Declaration

A paper has been produced from a previous version of chapter 2 and published as Merzoni, G. (2000) "Strategic Delegation in Cournot Oligopoly with Incomplete Information" in Baye, M. (ed.) *Advances in Applied Microeconomics. Vol. 9: Industrial Organisation*, pp.279-305, Amsterdam - New York, Jai Press-Elsevier Science.

A paper has been produced from a previous version of chapter 4 and published as Merzoni, G. (2000) "Natura del sindacato, delega dell'autorità e contrattazione", *Economia Politica*, vol.XVII, pp. 69-91, Aprile, n.1, Il Mulino, Bologna.

List of figures

List of tables

Druck und Bindung: Strauss Offsetdruck GmbH